100 Best Fresh Salad Recipes

100 Best Fresh Salad Recipes

100 REVITALIZING AND DELICIOUS RECIPES FOR A HEALTHY DIET

This edition published by
Cottage Door Press, LLC, in 2019.
First published 2010 by Parragon Books, Ltd.

5005 Newport Drive, Rolling Meadows, Illinois 60008

Photography by Günter Beer
Home Economist Stevan Paul
Design by Talking Design
Introduction and additional recipes
written by Beverly Le Blanc
The cover shows Avocado Hero Salad (42).

ISBN: 978-1-68052-899-2

Printed in China

Love Food™ is an imprint of Cottage Door Press, LLC. Parragon Books® and the Parragon® logo are registered trademarks of Cottage Door Press, LLC.

Notes for the Reader

This book uses standard kitchen measuring spoons and cups. All spoon and cup measurements are level unless otherwise indicated. Unless otherwise stated, milk is assumed to be whole, eggs are large, individual vegetables are medium, and pepper is freshly ground black pepper. Unless otherwise stated, all root vegetables should be peeled prior to using. People with nut allergies should be aware that some of the prepared ingredients used in the recipes in this book may contain nuts.

Garnishes, decorations, and serving suggestions are all optional and not necessarily included in the recipe ingredients or method. The times given are only an approximate guide. Preparation times differ according to the techniques used by different people and the cooking times may also vary from those given. Optional ingredients, variations, or serving suggestions have not been included in the time calculations.

contents

The taste of summer all year round

Take a fresh look at salads and you'll see there are a lot of exciting developments in the salad bowl. Banished forever is the image of salads as dull diet food consisting of little more than limp lettuce and soggy, flavorless tomatoes.

Today, salads are one of the ultimate health foods. They can contain an exciting variety of colorful, delicious, and satisfying ingredients that provide the nutrients essential for healthy living. You'll find plenty of inspiration in this book for a cornucopia of healthy salads for all occasions, from light lunches and family meals to stylish dinner parties. And remember, salads aren't just for summer. We have plenty of ideas for salads that brighten and lighten winter mealtimes, too. In fact, once you get into the habit of thinking "salad" while menu planning, ideas will come to you during any time of year as you push your shopping cart along the supermarket aisles or stop at the cheese counter or produce department.

Salads are versatile enough to cater to vegetarians and meat-eaters alike. Meat, seafood, and poultry are ideal salad ingredients, along with used lettuce and other leaves, vegetables, fruit, herbs, nuts, seeds, grains, legumes, and cheese. And with so many ingredients to choose from, salads can be as simple and light or complex and filling as you like. They also have the added bonus of being versatile enough to fit easily into all your meal plans, from first courses to desserts.

As you flip through these recipes you'll find classic favorites—Caesar salad, chef's salad, and tuna Niçoise, to name a few—as well as fresh, new ideas that capture the flavors of cuisines around the world. If, for example, the idea of chicken salad doesn't excite because you've been making the same recipe for as long as you can remember, try Thai-style chicken salad (page 102). You'll never think of chicken salad as humdrum again!

Bowls of Goodness

It wasn't long ago that "salads" and "health" were linked in the context of weight-loss and diets that were restrictive and ultimately unsatisfying. Today, however, salads are a delicious component of a healthy diet, giving you endless variety at mealtimes without long hours in the kitchen.

With fresh produce from all corners of the globe readily available in supermarkets and gourmet food stores, you can enjoy a variety of salads all year round.

We are all being urged to eat more fruit and vegetables every day, and a salad a day can go

a long way to help you meet the minimum target of 2½ cups for adults. Enjoy a bowl of traditional Greek salad (page 17) or caprese salad (page 34), for example, and you'll be more than halfway to success. What could be easier—or more enjoyable?

Salads also make great accompaniments, served alongside a filling bowl of pasta or a plate of hot or cold roast meat.

So, if you regularly fall back on the old favorite of just tossing a few green leaves with a simple oil-and-vinegar dressing, it's definitely time to think again. It's very easy to mix and match ingredients, and the choice has never been greater. And don't make the mistake of thinking all salad ingredients have to be raw, either. Adding small amounts of cooked meat, poultry, and seafood to lettuce and other vegetables gives you a satisfying meal. If you want a meal-in-a-bowl, try roast pork with pumpkin (page 113), smoked chicken salad with avocado & tarragon dressing (page 110), and shrimp & rice salad (page 135), for example. There are plenty of vegetarian main-course salads, too, such as the Middle Eastern favorite tabbouleh salad (page 190) and buckwheat noodle and smoked tofu salad (page 193).

Cooked vegetables also make good salad ingredients. Grilled peppers, fried eggplants, blanched beans of all varieties, and peas are just some of the cooked vegetables you'll find can add flavor and an extra dimension to the salads in this book.

Colorful Greens

Even with so many ingredients to choose from, salad greens still provide the backbone of many popular salads. Take a look around your supermarket and you'll see leaves in many colors and textures, ranging from white endive to bright red and white radicchio. They also have a variety of flavors, from robust and peppery to sweet, nutty, and mild.

The greater the variety of leaves you include in your salad, the more interesting it will be, and the more nutrients it will contain. When you select salad leaves, remember that the darker colored ones, such as spinach leaves, contain more beta-carotene, which help fight some forms of cancer and other illnesses. Leafy green vegetables are also excellent sources of fiber.

It's become very convenient to grab a bag of mixed salad leaves at the supermarket, but it can be more satisfying to sample a selection of greens sold separately at farmers markets. Asian and other ethnic food stores are also a good place to find unusual greens.

Try these fresh and crisp greens to add variety to your salad bowl:

• Arugula—known for its pronounced peppery flavor, these dark green leaves perk up many salads. Popular in Italian salads. Substitute watercress if you can't find arugula.

• Beet greens—distinctive with their red stems, these soft leaves are mildly flavored.

• Mâche—also labeled as corn salad or lamb's lettuce, these tender leaves have a mild, slightly nutty flavor.

• Mesclun or mesclum—now sold in supermarkets, this French mix of leaves can include arugula, chervil, dandelion, and oak-leaf lettuce. Just add dressing and toss.

• Mizuna—from the Far East, this winter green has a full peppery flavor. Its pointy green leaves add visual interest to salads, too.

• Nasturtium—use both the colorful flowers and peppery leaves in salads.

• Radicchio—there is nothing like the bright red and white leaves of this member of the bitter endive family to liven autumn and early winter salads. It has a crisp texture and nutty, peppery flavor.

• Red chard—like beet greens, these fiber-rich leaves have bright red stems and sometimes the leaves are tinged red as well.

• Romaine lettuce—Caesar salad (page 14) simply wouldn't be Caesar salad without these long, crisp leaves. Comes in a large, compact head with long, crisp leaves that have a sweet nutty flavor.

Keep It Fresh

Good salads are made with good ingredients, and freshness is all-important when buying salad greens. Because of the leaves' high water content, they are very perishable, so buy them as close as possible to serving. Not only will they taste best, they contain the most nutrients when they are in peak condition.

Let your eyes guide you when shopping for salad greens—fresh leaves look fresh. They won't have any leaves tinged with brown, nor will they be wilted or slimy.

When you get salad ingredients home, give them a rinse in cold water, then spin them dry or use a tea cloth to pat them dry. Never leave them to soak in a sink full of cold water because all the water-soluble vitamins and minerals will drain out.

Use leafy ingredients as soon as possible, but most will keep for up to four days in a sealed container in the refrigerator. Once you open bags of prepared leaves, however, they should be used within 24 hours. You can prepare salad greens several hours in advance and store in the refrigerator, but do not dress until just before serving because the acid in most dressings causes the leaves to wilt and become unappetizing.

sunshine

a collection of vegetable salads

Caesar salad

serves 4

ingredients

2/3 cup olive oil

2 garlic cloves

5 slices white bread, crusts removed, cut into 1/2-inch cubes

1 large egg

2 romaine lettuces or 3 Boston lettuces

2 tbsp lemon juice

salt and pepper, to taste

8 canned anchovy fillets, drained and coarsely chopped

3/4 cup fresh Parmesan cheese shavings

Bring a small, heavy-bottom pan of water to a boil.

Meanwhile, to make the croutons, heat 4 tablespoons of the olive oil in a heavy-bottom skillet. Add the garlic and cubed bread and cook, stirring and tossing frequently, for 4–5 minutes, or until the bread is crispy and golden all over. Remove from the skillet with a slotted spoon and drain on paper towels.

Add the egg to the boiling water and cook for 1 minute, then remove from the pan and set aside.

To make the dressing, mix the remaining olive oil and lemon juice together, then season with salt and pepper. Crack the egg into the dressing, and whisk to blend.

Arrange the salad greens in a serving bowl. Pour the dressing over the salad, toss well, then add the croutons and chopped anchovies and toss the salad again. Sprinkle with Parmesan cheese shavings and serve.

traditional Greek salad

serves 4

ingredients

½ head of iceberg lettuce or 1 lettuce such as romaine or escarole, shredded or sliced
4 tomatoes, cut into fourths
½ cucumber, sliced
7 oz feta cheese, cut into 1-inch cubes
12 Greek black olives, pitted
2 tbsp chopped fresh herbs, such as oregano, flat-leaf parsley, mint, or basil

for the dressing

6 tbsp extra-virgin olive oil
2 tbsp fresh lemon juice
1 garlic clove, crushed
pinch of sugar
salt and pepper, to taste

Make the dressing by whisking together the olive oil, lemon juice, garlic, sugar, salt, and pepper in a small bowl. Set aside.

Put the lettuce, tomatoes, and cucumber in a salad bowl. Scatter the feta cheese on top, and toss together.

Just before serving, whisk the dressing, pour over the salad greens, and toss together. Garnish with the olives and chopped herbs, and serve.

mozzarella salad with sun-dried tomatoes

serves 4

ingredients

3½ oz mixed salad greens, such as oak leaf lettuce, baby spinach, and arugula

1 lb 2 oz smoked mozzarella cheese, sliced

for the dressing

5 oz sun-dried tomatoes in olive oil (drained weight), reserving the oil from the jar

¼ cup coarsely shredded fresh basil

¼ cup coarsely chopped fresh flat-leaf parsley

1 tbsp capers, rinsed

1 tbsp balsamic vinegar

1 garlic clove, coarsely chopped

extra olive oil, if necessary

pepper, to taste

To make the dressing, put the sun-dried tomatoes, basil, parsley, capers, balsamic vinegar, and garlic in a food processor or blender. Measure the oil from the sun-dried tomatoes jar and make it up to ⅔ cup with more olive oil if necessary. Add it to the food processor or blender and process until smooth. Season with pepper.

Divide the salad greens among 4 individual serving plates. Top with the slices of mozzarella and spoon the dressing over them. Serve immediately.

red & green salad

serves 4

ingredients

3 tbsp extra-virgin olive oil

juice of 1 orange

1 tsp superfine sugar

1 tsp fennel seeds

salt and pepper, to taste

1 lb 7 oz cooked beets, diced

4 oz fresh baby spinach leaves

To make the dressing, heat the olive oil in a small, heavy-bottom pan. Add the orange juice, sugar, and fennel seeds and season with salt and pepper. Stir constantly until the sugar has dissolved.

Add the beets to the pan, and stir gently to coat. Remove the pan from the heat.

Arrange the baby spinach leaves in a large salad bowl. Spoon the warmed beets on top and serve immediately.

roasted garlic, sweet potato, broiled eggplant & bell pepper salad with mozzarella

serves 4

ingredients

2 sweet potatoes, peeled and cut into chunks

2 tbsp olive oil

pepper, to taste

2 garlic cloves, crushed

1 large eggplant, sliced

2 red bell peppers, seeded and sliced

7 oz mixed salad greens

11 oz fresh mozzarella cheese, drained and sliced

for the dressing

1 tbsp balsamic vinegar

1 garlic clove, crushed

3 tbsp olive oil

1 small shallot, finely chopped

2 tbsp chopped mixed fresh herbs, such as tarragon, chervil, and basil

pepper, to taste

Preheat the oven to 375°F. Put the sweet potato chunks into a roasting pan with the olive oil, pepper, and garlic, and toss to combine. Roast in the preheated oven for 30 minutes, or until soft and slightly charred.

Meanwhile, preheat the broiler to high. Arrange the eggplant and bell pepper slices on the broiler pan and cook under the preheated broiler, turning occasionally, for 10 minutes, or until soft and slightly charred.

To make the dressing, whisk the balsamic vinegar, garlic, and olive oil together in a small bowl, and stir in the shallot and herbs. Season with pepper.

To serve, divide the salad greens among 4 serving plates, and arrange the sweet potato, eggplant, bell peppers, and mozzarella on top. Drizzle with the dressing and serve.

mixed mushroom salad

serves 4

ingredients

3 tbsp pine nuts

2 red onions, cut into chunks

4 tbsp olive oil

2 garlic cloves, crushed

3 slices whole-wheat bread, cubed

7 oz mixed salad greens

9 oz cremini mushrooms, sliced

5½ oz shiitake mushrooms, sliced

5½ oz oyster mushrooms, torn

for the dressing

1 garlic clove, crushed

2 tbsp red wine vinegar

4 tbsp walnut oil

1 tbsp finely chopped fresh parsley

pepper, to taste

Preheat the oven to 350°F. Heat a nonstick skillet over medium heat, add the pine nuts, and cook, turning, until just browned. Tip into a bowl and set aside.

Put the onions and 1 tablespoon of the olive oil into a roasting pan and toss to coat. Roast in the preheated oven for 30 minutes.

Meanwhile, make the croutons by heating 1 tablespoon of the remaining oil with the garlic in the nonstick skillet over high heat. Add the bread and cook, turning frequently, for 5 minutes, or until brown and crisp. Remove from the skillet and set aside.

Divide the salad greens among 4 serving plates and add the roasted onions. To make the dressing, whisk the garlic, vinegar, and walnut oil together in a small bowl. Stir in the parsley and season with pepper. Drizzle over the salad and onions.

Heat the remaining oil in a skillet, add the cremini and shiitake mushrooms, and cook for 2–3 minutes, stirring frequently. Add the oyster mushrooms, and cook for an additional 2–3 minutes. Divide the hot mushroom mixture among the 4 plates. Sprinkle the pine nuts and croutons on top, and serve.

warm red lentil salad with goat cheese

serves 4

ingredients

2 tbsp olive oil

2 tsp cumin seeds

2 garlic cloves, crushed

2 tsp grated fresh gingerroot

1½ cups split red lentils

3 cups vegetable stock

2 tbsp chopped fresh mint

2 tbsp chopped fresh cilantro

2 red onions, thinly sliced

4½ cups baby spinach leaves

1 tsp hazelnut oil

5½ oz soft goat cheese

4 tbsp strained plain yogurt

pepper, to taste

Heat half the olive oil in a large skillet over medium heat, add the cumin seeds, garlic, and gingerroot, and cook for 2 minutes, stirring constantly.

Stir in the lentils, then add the stock, a ladleful at a time, until it is all absorbed, stirring constantly—this will take about 20 minutes. Remove from the heat, and stir in the mint and cilantro.

Meanwhile, heat the remaining olive oil in a skillet over medium heat, add the onions, and cook, stirring frequently, for 10 minutes, or until soft and lightly browned.

Toss the spinach in the hazelnut oil in a bowl, then divide among 4 serving plates.

Mash the goat cheese with the yogurt in a small bowl, and season with pepper.

Divide the lentils among the serving plates, and top with the onions and goat cheese mixture.

green bean & walnut salad

serves 2

ingredients

1 lb green beans
1 small onion, finely chopped
1 garlic clove, chopped
4 tbsp freshly grated Parmesan cheese
2 tbsp chopped walnuts or almonds, to garnish

for the dressing

6 tbsp olive oil
2 tbsp white wine vinegar
salt and pepper, to taste
2 tsp chopped fresh tarragon

Trim the beans, but leave them whole. Cook for 3–4 minutes in boiling salted water. Drain well, rinse under cold running water, and drain again. Put into a mixing bowl, and add the onion, garlic, and cheese.

Place the dressing ingredients in a jar with a screw-top lid. Shake well. Pour the dressing over the salad and toss gently to coat. Cover with plastic wrap, and chill for at least 30 minutes. Remove the beans from the refrigerator 10 minutes before serving. Give them a quick stir and transfer to serving bowls.

Toast the nuts in a dry skillet over medium heat for 2 minutes, or until they begin to brown. Sprinkle the toasted nuts over the beans to garnish before serving.

red onion, tomato & herb salad

serves 4

ingredients

2 lb tomatoes, thinly sliced
1 tbsp sugar (optional)
salt and pepper, to taste
1 red onion, thinly sliced
large handful coarsely chopped fresh herbs, such as tarragon, sorrel, cilantro, or basil

for the dressing

2–4 tbsp vegetable oil
2 tbsp red wine vinegar or fruit vinegar

Arrange the tomato slices in a shallow bowl. Sprinkle with sugar (if using), salt, and pepper.

Separate the onion slices into rings, and sprinkle them over the tomatoes. Sprinkle the herbs over the top.

Place the dressing ingredients in a jar with a screw-top lid. Shake well. Pour the dressing over the salad, and mix gently.

Cover with plastic wrap and chill for 20 minutes. Remove the salad from the refrigerator 5 minutes before serving.

nutty beet salad

serves 4

ingredients

3 tbsp red wine vinegar or fruit vinegar
3 cooked beets, grated
2 sharp eating apples
2 tbsp lemon juice
4 large handfuls mixed salad greens, to serve
4 tbsp pecans, to garnish

for the dressing

1/4 cup plain yogurt
1/4 cup mayonnaise
1 garlic clove, chopped
1 tbsp chopped fresh dill
salt and pepper, to taste

Sprinkle vinegar over the beets, cover with plastic wrap, and chill for at least 4 hours.

Core and slice the apples, place the slices in a dish, and sprinkle with the lemon juice to prevent discoloration.

Combine the dressing ingredients in a small bowl. Remove the beets from the refrigerator and dress. Add the apples to the beets, and mix gently to coat with the salad dressing.

To serve, arrange a handful of salad greens on each plate and top with a large spoonful of the apple and beet mixture.

Toast the pecans in a heavy, dry skillet over medium heat for 2 minutes, or until they begin to brown. Sprinkle them over the salad to garnish.

caprese salad

serves 4

ingredients

10 oz buffalo mozzarella, drained and thinly sliced

8 large tomatoes, sliced

20 fresh basil leaves

½ cup extra-virgin olive oil

salt and pepper, to taste

Arrange the mozzarella and tomato slices on 4 individual serving plates and season with salt. Refrigerate for 30 minutes.

Sprinkle the basil leaves over the salad, and drizzle with the olive oil. Season with pepper, and serve immediately.

broiled bell pepper salad

serves 4–6

ingredients

6 large red, orange, or yellow bell peppers, each cut in half lengthwise, de-seeded, broiled, and skinned
4 hard-boiled eggs, shelled and cut into wedges
12 anchovy fillets in oil, drained
12 large black olives, pitted
extra-virgin olive oil or garlic-flavored olive oil, for drizzling
sherry vinegar, to taste
salt and pepper, to taste

Cut the broiled bell peppers into thin strips. Arrange on a serving platter.

Arrange the eggs over the bell pepper strips, along with the anchovy fillets and olives.

Drizzle oil over the top, then splash with sherry vinegar, adding both to taste. Sprinkle a little salt and pepper over the top and serve.

tomato salad with feta cheese

serves 4

ingredients

12 plum tomatoes, sliced

1 very small red onion, thinly sliced

½ oz arugula leaves

20 black olives, pitted

1 egg

3 tbsp all-purpose flour

7 oz feta cheese, cut into 1-inch cubes

2 tbsp olive oil

for the dressing

3 tbsp extra-virgin olive oil

juice of ½ lemon

2 tsp chopped fresh oregano

pinch of sugar

pepper, to taste

Make the dressing by whisking together the extra-virgin olive oil, lemon juice, oregano, sugar, and pepper in a pitcher or small bowl. Set aside.

Prepare the salad by arranging the tomatoes, onion, arugula, and olives on 4 individual plates.

Beat the egg in a dish and put the flour on a separate plate. Coat the feta cheese in the egg, shake off the excess, and then coat in the flour.

Heat the olive oil in a large skillet, add the cheese, and cook over medium heat, turning the cubes of cheese until they are golden on all sides.

Scatter the fried feta over the salad. Whisk together the prepared dressing, spoon over the salad, and serve warm.

broiled bell pepper & goat cheese salad

serves 4

ingredients

2 red bell peppers

2 green bell peppers

2 yellow or orange bell peppers

½ cup vinaigrette or herb vinaigrette

6 scallions, finely chopped

1 tbsp capers in brine, rinsed

7 oz soft goat cheese, any rind removed

fresh flat-leaf parsley, chopped, to garnish

Preheat the broiler to high. Arrange the bell peppers on a broiler pan, position about 4 inches from the heat, and broil for 8–10 minutes, turning them frequently, until the skins are charred all over. Transfer the bell peppers to a bowl, cover with a damp dish towel, and let stand until cool enough to handle.

Using a small knife, skin each of the bell peppers. Working over a bowl to catch the juices from inside the bell peppers, cut each one in half and remove the cores and seeds, then cut the flesh into thin strips.

Arrange the bell peppers on a serving platter and spoon over the reserved juices, then add the vinaigrette. Sprinkle over the scallions and capers, then crumble the cheese on top. If not serving immediately, cover with plastic wrap and chill until required. Garnish with parsley to serve.

avocado hero salad

serves 2

ingredients

2/3 cup dry green peas suitable for sprouting
2/3 cup whole quinoa seeds suitable for sprouting
2/3 cup baby spinach
2/3 cup baby asparagus tips
16 baby plum tomatoes
1/4 cup fresh watercress
2 ripe avocados, pitted, peeled, and sliced into bite-sized pieces
2 1/2 tbsp raw pine nuts
8 fresh basil sprigs
1/2 tbsp cold-pressed extra-virgin olive oil

for the dressing

2 1/2 tbsp cold-pressed extra-virgin olive oil
1/2 tbsp raw wine vinegar
2 1/2 tsp raw honey
1 1/4 tsp stone-ground mustard
1/2 tsp sea salt
1/2 tsp pepper

To sprout the peas, put them in a wide-necked glass jar and soak them overnight in tepid water, covered with muslin or a similar material. In the morning, drain and rinse the peas, and fill the jar with fresh water. Drain and rinse the peas twice a day for 5 days, until they have sprouted. Rinse and drain to use.

To sprout the quinoa, use the same method as the peas but soak them for only 4 hours. They will sprout in about 2 days.

Arrange the spinach, all but four of the asparagus tips, and the plum tomatoes in two serving dishes with most of the watercress.

Arrange three quarters of the avocado slices in the dishes with the remaining watercress and the sprouted peas and quinoa. Sprinkle three-quarters of the pine nuts on top.

In a small bowl, mash the remaining avocado with the remaining pine nuts, six of the basil sprigs, and the half tablespoon of olive oil until you have a rough puree.

Make the dressing by thoroughly combining the ingredients in a small dish. Spoon most of this over the salad.

Finish the salad by arranging two asparagus tips in the center of each dish, followed by half the avocado puree and a basil sprig. Drizzle the rest of the dressing on top to serve.

Mexican tomato salad

serves 4

ingredients

1 lb 5 oz tomatoes, peeled, seeded, and coarsely chopped

1 onion, thinly sliced and pushed out into rings

14 oz canned kidney beans, drained and rinsed

for the dressing

1 fresh green chili, seeded and diced

3 tbsp chopped fresh cilantro

3 tbsp olive oil

1 garlic clove, finely chopped

4 tbsp lime juice

salt and pepper, to taste

Place the chopped tomatoes and onion slices in a large serving bowl, and mix well. Stir in the kidney beans.

To make the dressing, mix the chili, cilantro, olive oil, garlic, and lime juice together in a measuring cup and season with salt and pepper.

Pour the dressing over the salad and toss thoroughly. Serve immediately, or cover with plastic wrap and let chill in the refrigerator until required.

Thai noodle salad

serves 4

ingredients

1 oz dried wood ear mushrooms

2 oz dried Chinese mushrooms

4 oz cellophane noodles

½ cup cooked lean ground pork

4 oz shelled raw shrimp

5 fresh red chilies, seeded and thinly sliced

1 tbsp chopped fresh cilantro

3 tbsp Thai fish sauce

3 tbsp lime juice

1 tbsp brown sugar

Put the wood ear and Chinese mushrooms in separate bowls and pour enough boiling water over each to cover. Let soak for 30 minutes. Put the cellophane noodles in a separate bowl, and pour enough hot water on top to cover. Let the noodles soak for 10 minutes, or according to the package instructions.

Drain the wood ear mushrooms, rinse thoroughly, and cut into small pieces. Drain the Chinese mushrooms, squeezing out as much liquid as possible. Cut off and discard the stalks, and cut the caps in half. Drain the noodles and cut them into short lengths with scissors.

Pour just enough water into a pan to cover the bottom and bring to a boil. Add the pork, shrimp, wood ear and Chinese mushrooms, and let simmer, stirring, for 3 minutes, or until cooked through. Drain well.

Put the chilies, cilantro, fish sauce, lime juice, and brown sugar in a salad bowl, and stir until the sugar has dissolved. Add the noodles and the shrimp and pork mixture, toss well, and serve.

sweet potato & bean salad

serves 4

ingredients

1 sweet potato, peeled and diced
4 baby carrots, halved lengthwise
4 tomatoes, de-seeded and chopped
4 celery stalks, chopped
8 oz canned cranberry beans, drained and rinsed
4 oz mixed salad greens, such as frisée, arugula, radicchio, and oak leaf lettuce
1 tbsp golden raisins
4 scallions, sliced diagonally

for the dressing

2 tbsp lemon juice
1 garlic clove, crushed
5 fl oz plain yogurt
2 tbsp olive oil
salt and pepper, to taste

Bring a pan of water to a boil over medium heat. Add the sweet potato, and cook for 10 minutes, until tender. Drain the water, transfer to a bowl, and set aside.

Cook the carrots in a separate pan of boiling water for 1 minute. Drain thoroughly and add to the sweet potato. Add the tomatoes to a bowl with the celery and beans. Mix well.

Line a large serving bowl with the mixed salad greens. Spoon the sweet potato and bean mixture on top, then sprinkle with golden raisins and scallions.

Put all the dressing ingredients in a screw-top jar, and shake until well blended. Pour over the salad, and serve.

raspberry & feta salad with couscous

serves 6

ingredients

$2\frac{1}{2}$ cups chicken stock or vegetable stock

12 oz couscous

8 oz feta cheese, cubed or crumbled

2 zucchini, thinly sliced

4 scallions, trimmed and diagonally sliced

12 oz fresh raspberries

$\frac{1}{3}$ cup pine nuts, toasted

small bunch of fresh basil

grated rind of 1 lemon

for the dressing

1 tbsp white wine vinegar

1 tbsp balsamic vinegar

4 tbsp extra-virgin olive oil

juice of 1 lemon

salt and pepper, to taste

Bring the stock to a boil. Put the couscous in a large heatproof bowl, and pour over the stock. Stir well, then cover and let soak until all the stock has been absorbed.

Transfer the couscous to a large serving bowl, and stir well to break up any lumps. Add the cheese, zucchini, scallions, raspberries, and pine nuts. Stir in the basil and lemon rind and gently toss all the ingredients together.

Put all the dressing ingredients in a screw-top jar and shake until well blended. Pour over the salad and serve.

orecchiette salad with pears & blue cheese

serves 4

ingredients

9 oz dried orecchiette

1 head radicchio, torn into pieces

1 oak leaf lettuce, torn into pieces

2 pears, diced

1 tbsp lemon juice

9 oz blue cheese, diced

½ cup chopped walnuts

4 tomatoes, quartered

1 red onion, sliced

1 carrot, grated

8 fresh basil leaves

2 oz canned or frozen corn kernels

for the dressing

4 tbsp olive oil

2 tbsp lemon juice

salt and pepper, to taste

Bring a large heavy-bottom pan of lightly salted water to a boil. Add the pasta, return to a boil, and cook for 8–10 minutes, or until tender but still firm to the bite. Drain, rinse in a bowl of cold water, and drain again.

Place the radicchio and oak leaf lettuce leaves in a large bowl. Toss the diced pear with 1 tablespoon of lemon juice in a small bowl to prevent discoloration. Top the salad with the blue cheese, walnuts, pears, pasta, tomatoes, onion slices, and grated carrot. Add the basil and corn.

For the dressing, mix the lemon juice and the olive oil together in a measuring cup, then season with salt and pepper. Pour the dressing over the salad, toss, and serve.

vegetable salad with garlic dressing

serves 4

ingredients

3 oz cucumber, cut into batons

6 scallions, halved

2 tomatoes, seeded and cut into 8 wedges

1 yellow bell pepper, seeded and cut into strips

2 celery stalks, cut into strips

4 radishes, quartered

3 oz arugula

1 tbsp chopped fresh mint, to garnish (optional)

for the dressing

2 tbsp lemon juice

1 garlic clove, crushed

2/3 cup plain yogurt

2 tbsp olive oil

salt and pepper, to taste

To make the salad, gently mix the cucumber, scallions, tomato wedges, yellow bell pepper strips, celery strips, radishes, and arugula in a large serving bowl.

To make the dressing, stir the lemon juice, garlic, yogurt, and olive oil together in a small bowl until thoroughly combined. Season with salt and pepper.

Spoon the dressing over the salad and toss to mix. Sprinkle the salad with chopped mint (if using), and serve.

warm pasta salad

serves 4

ingredients

8 oz dried farfalle

6 pieces of sun-dried tomato in oil, drained and chopped

4 scallions, chopped

1¼ cups arugula, shredded

½ cucumber, seeded and diced

salt and pepper, to taste

for the dressing

4 tbsp olive oil

1 tbsp white wine vinegar

½ tsp superfine sugar

1 tsp dijon mustard

salt and pepper, to taste

4 fresh basil leaves, finely shredded

To make the dressing, whisk the olive oil, vinegar, sugar, and mustard together in a bowl or pitcher. Season with salt and pepper, and stir in the basil.

Bring a large heavy-bottom pan of lightly salted water to a boil. Add the pasta, return to a boil, and cook for 8–10 minutes, or until tender but still firm to the bite. Drain and transfer to a salad bowl. Add the dressing, and toss well.

Add the tomatoes, scallions, arugula, and cucumber, season with salt and pepper, and toss. Serve warm.

Italian salad

serves 4

ingredients

8 oz dried conchiglie

1¾ oz pine nuts

12 oz cherry tomatoes, cut in half

1 red bell pepper, seeded and cut into bite-size chunks

1 red onion, chopped

7 oz buffalo mozzarella, cubed

12 black olives, pitted

1 oz fresh basil leaves

shavings of fresh Parmesan cheese, to garnish

crusty bread, to serve

for the dressing

5 tbsp extra-virgin olive oil

2 tbsp balsamic vinegar

1 tbsp chopped fresh basil

salt and pepper, to taste

Bring a large pan of lightly salted water to a boil. Add the pasta, and cook over medium heat for about 10 minutes, or according to the package instructions. When cooked, the pasta should be tender but still firm to the bite. Drain, rinse under cold running water, and drain again. Let cool.

While the pasta is cooking, put the pine nuts in a dry skillet and cook over low heat for 1–2 minutes, until golden brown. Remove from the heat, transfer to a dish, and let cool.

To make the dressing, put the olive oil, balsamic vinegar, and basil into a small bowl. Season with salt and pepper and stir together well. Cover with plastic wrap, and set aside.

To assemble the salad, divide the pasta among 4 serving bowls. Add the pine nuts, tomatoes, red bell pepper, onion, cheese, and olives. Scatter over the basil leaves, then drizzle over the dressing. Garnish with fresh Parmesan cheese shavings and serve with crusty bread.

potato salad

serves 4

ingredients

1 lb 9 oz new potatoes

1 cup mayonnaise

1 tsp paprika

salt and pepper, to taste

8 scallions, thinly sliced

2 tbsp snipped fresh chives

pinch of paprika, to garnish

Bring a large pan of lightly salted water to a boil. Add the potatoes and cook for 10–15 minutes, or until just tender.

Drain the potatoes and rinse them under cold running water until completely cold. Transfer the potatoes to a bowl and set aside until required.

Mix the mayonnaise, paprika, and salt and pepper together in a bowl. Pour the mixture over the potatoes. Add the scallions to the potatoes, and toss together.

Transfer the potato salad to a serving bowl, and sprinkle with snipped chives and a pinch of paprika. Cover and let chill in the refrigerator until required.

warm Capri salad

serves 4

ingredients

2 beefsteak tomatoes, cut into thin slices
4½ oz mozzarella cheese,
  drained and sliced
12 black olives, pitted and sliced
8 fresh basil leaves
1 tbsp balsamic vinegar
1 tbsp extra-virgin olive oil
salt and pepper, to taste
fresh basil leaves, to garnish

Preheat the broiler. Layer the tomatoes, mozzarella slices, olives, and basil leaves in 4 stacks, finishing with a layer of cheese on top.

Place each stack under the hot broiler for 2–3 minutes or just long enough to melt the mozzarella.

Drizzle the balsamic vinegar and olive oil on top, and season with a little salt and pepper.

Transfer to individual serving plates, and garnish with fresh basil leaves. Serve immediately.

hearty

a collection of meat & poultry salads

Waldorf summer chicken salad

serves 4

ingredients

1 lb 2 oz red dessert apples, diced

3 tbsp fresh lemon juice

2/3 cup light mayonnaise

1 head celery, thinly sliced

4 shallots, sliced

1 garlic clove, finely chopped

3/4 cup walnuts, chopped

1 lb 2 oz cooked chicken, cubed

1 romaine lettuce

pepper, to taste

Place the apples in a bowl with the lemon juice and 1 tablespoon of mayonnaise. Refrigerate for 40 minutes.

Add the celery, shallots, and garlic to the apple, and mix together. Add the walnuts, reserving about 1 tablespoon for garnish. Stir in the remaining mayonnaise, and blend thoroughly.

Add the cooked chicken to the bowl and mix well.

Line serving bowls with the lettuce. Pile the chicken salad on top, sprinkle with pepper, and garnish with the remaining chopped walnuts.

chef's salad

serves 6

ingredients

1 iceberg lettuce, shredded
6 oz cooked lean ham, cut into thin strips
6 oz roast beef, cut into thin strips
12 oz cooked chicken, cut into thin strips
6 oz gruyère cheese, cubed
4 tomatoes, quartered
3 hard-boiled eggs, shelled and quartered
1¾ cups thousand island dressing
sliced french bread, to serve

Arrange the lettuce on a large serving platter. Arrange the cold meats on top.

Arrange the gruyère over the salad, and place the tomato and egg quarters around the edge of the platter. Serve the salad immediately with the thousand island dressing and sliced french bread.

prosciutto with melon & asparagus

serves 4

ingredients

8 oz asparagus spears

1 small or ½ medium-size galia or cantaloupe melon, cut into wedges

2 oz prosciutto, thinly sliced

5½ oz bag mixed salad greens, such as herb salad with arugula

½ cup fresh raspberries

1 tbsp freshly shaved Parmesan cheese

for the dressing

1 tbsp balsamic vinegar

2 tbsp raspberry vinegar

2 tbsp orange juice

Trim the asparagus, cutting in half if very long. Cook in lightly salted boiling water over medium heat for 5 minutes, or until tender. Drain and plunge into cold water, then drain again and set aside.

Separate the prosciutto slices, cut in half, and wrap around the melon wedges.

Arrange the salad greens on a large serving platter, and place the melon wedges on top together with the asparagus spears. Scatter the raspberries and Parmesan shavings on top.

Place the vinegars and juice in a screw-top jar, and shake until blended. Pour over the salad, and serve.

warm beef Niçoise

serves 4

ingredients

4 tenderloin steaks, about 4 oz each, fat discarded
2 tbsp red wine vinegar
2 tbsp orange juice
2 tsp dijon mustard
2 eggs
6 oz new potatoes
4 oz green beans, trimmed
6 oz mixed salad greens, such as baby spinach, arugula, and mizuna
1 yellow bell pepper, seeded, peeled, and cut into strips
6 oz cherry tomatoes, halved
black olives, pitted, to garnish
2 tsp extra-virgin olive oil

Place the steaks in a shallow dish. Blend the vinegar with 1 tablespoon of orange juice and 1 teaspoon of mustard. Pour over the steaks, cover, then let stand in the refrigerator for at least 30 minutes, turning over halfway through the marinating time.

Place the eggs in a pan, and cover with cold water. Bring to a boil, then reduce the heat to a simmer and cook for 10 minutes. Remove and place the eggs into cold water. Once cold, shell and set aside.

Meanwhile, place the potatoes in a pan and cover with cold water. Bring to a boil, then cover and let simmer for 15 minutes, or until tender when pierced with a fork. Drain and set aside.

Bring a saucepan of water to a boil, add the beans and cook for 5 minutes, or until just tender. Drain, plunge into cold water, and drain again. Arrange the potatoes and beans on top of the salad leaves with the bell pepper, cherry tomatoes, and olives. Blend the remaining orange juice and mustard with the olive oil and set aside.

Heat a stove top grill pan or griddle until smoking. Drain the steaks and cook for 3–5 minutes on each side or according to personal preference. Slice the steaks and arrange on top of the salad, then pour over the dressing and serve.

Cajun chicken salad

serves 4

ingredients

4 skinless, boneless chicken breasts, about 5 oz each
4 tsp Cajun seasoning
2 tsp vegetable oil (optional)
1 ripe mango, peeled, seeded, and cut into thick slices
7 oz mixed salad greens
1 red onion, thinly sliced and cut in half
6 oz cooked beet, diced
3 oz radishes, sliced
generous 3/8 cup walnut halves
2 tbsp sesame seeds, to garnish

for the dressing

4 tbsp walnut oil
1–2 tsp dijon mustard
1 tbsp lemon juice
salt and pepper, to taste

Make 3 diagonal slashes across each chicken breast. Put the chicken into a shallow dish and sprinkle all over with the Cajun seasoning. Cover and let chill for at least 30 minutes.

When ready to cook, brush a stove-top grill pan with the vegetable oil, if using. Heat over high heat until very hot and a few drops of water sprinkled into the pan sizzle immediately. Add the chicken and cook for 7–8 minutes on each side, or until thoroughly cooked. If still slightly pink in the center, cook a little longer. Remove the chicken and set aside.

Add the mango slices to the pan, and cook for 2 minutes on each side. Remove and set aside.

Meanwhile, arrange the salad greens in a salad bowl and toss in the onion, beet, radishes, and walnut halves.

To make the dressing, put the walnut oil, mustard, lemon juice, and salt and pepper in a screw-top jar, and shake until well blended. Pour over the salad.

Arrange the mango and the salad on the serving plate, top with the chicken breast, and garnish with sesame seeds.

roast beef salad

serves 4

ingredients

1 lb 10 oz beef fillet, trimmed of any visible fat
pepper, to taste
2 tsp Worcestershire sauce
3 tbsp olive oil
14 oz green beans
3½ oz small pasta, such as pipe rigate or orecchiette
2 red onions, finely sliced
1 large head radicchio
generous ¼ cup green olives, pitted
⅓ cup shelled hazelnuts, whole

for the dressing

1 tsp dijon mustard
2 tbsp white wine vinegar
5 tbsp olive oil

Preheat the oven to 425°F. Rub the beef with pepper and Worcestershire sauce. Heat 2 tablespoons of the olive oil in a small roasting pan over high heat, add the beef, and sear on all sides. Transfer the dish to the preheated oven and roast for 30 minutes. Remove and let cool.

Bring a large pan of water to a boil, add the green beans, and cook for 5 minutes, or until just tender. Remove with a slotted spoon and rinse the beans under cold running water. Drain and put into a large bowl.

Return the bean cooking water to a boil, add the pasta, and cook for 11 minutes, or until tender. Drain, return to the pan, and toss with the remaining oil.

Add the pasta to the beans with the onions, radicchio leaves, olives, and hazelnuts. Mix gently, and transfer to a serving bowl or dish. Arrange some thinly sliced beef on top.

Whisk the dressing ingredients together in a separate bowl, then pour over the salad, and serve immediately.

walnut, pear & crispy bacon salad

serves 4

ingredients

4 lean bacon slices
⅔ cup walnut halves
2 red bartlett pears, cored and sliced lengthwise
1 tbsp lemon juice
6 oz watercress, tough stalks removed

for the dressing

3 tbsp extra-virgin olive oil
2 tbsp lemon juice
½ tsp honey
salt and pepper, to taste

Cook the bacon in a frying pan until crispy. Let cool, then cut into ½-inch pieces.

Meanwhile, heat a dry skillet over medium heat, and lightly toast the walnuts, shaking the skillet frequently, for 3 minutes, or until lightly browned. Let cool.

Toss the pears in the lemon juice to prevent discoloration. Put the watercress, walnuts, pears, and bacon into a salad bowl.

To make the dressing, whisk the olive oil, lemon juice, and honey together in a small bowl or pitcher. Season with salt and pepper, then pour over the salad. Toss well to combine and serve.

warm chicken liver salad

serves 4

ingredients

salad greens
1 tbsp olive oil
1 small onion, finely chopped
1 lb frozen chicken livers, thawed
1 tsp chopped fresh tarragon
1 tsp whole-grain mustard
2 tbsp balsamic vinegar
salt and pepper, to taste

Arrange the salad greens on serving plates.

Heat the olive oil in a nonstick skillet, add the onion, and cook for 5 minutes, or until softened. Add the chicken livers, tarragon, and mustard and cook for 3–5 minutes, stirring, until tender. Place on top of the salad greens.

Add the vinegar, salt, and pepper to the skillet and heat, stirring constantly, to deglaze the skillet. Pour the dressing over the chicken livers, and serve warm.

artichoke & prosciutto salad

serves 4

ingredients

9¾ oz canned artichoke hearts in oil, drained, and quartered
4 small tomatoes, cut into wedges
1 oz sun-dried tomatoes in oil, drained and thinly sliced
1½ oz prosciutto, cut into thin strips
1 tbsp pitted black olives, halved
handful of fresh basil sprigs
crusty bread, to serve (optional)

for the dressing

3 tbsp olive oil
1 tbsp white wine vinegar
1 garlic clove, crushed
½ tsp mild mustard
1 tsp honey
salt and pepper, to taste

Combine the artichoke hearts, fresh tomatoes, sun-dried tomatoes, prosciutto, and olive halves in a bowl.

Keeping a few basil sprigs whole for garnishing, tear the remainder of the leaves into small pieces, and add to the bowl containing the other salad ingredients.

To make the dressing, place all the dressing ingredients in a screw-top jar, and shake vigorously until they are well blended.

Pour the dressing over the salad and toss together. Garnish the salad with a few basil sprigs, and serve with crusty bread, if desired.

lima bean, onion & herb salad with spicy sausage

serves 2

ingredients

1 tbsp vegetable oil
1 small onion, finely sliced
9 oz canned lima beans, drained and rinsed
1 tsp balsamic vinegar
2 chorizo sausages, sliced diagonally
1 small tomato, diced
2 tbsp harissa paste
3 oz mixed herb salad

Heat the oil in a nonstick skillet over medium heat, add the onion, and cook, stirring frequently, until softened but not browned. Add the beans and cook for an additional 1 minute, then add the balsamic vinegar, stirring well. Keep warm.

Meanwhile, heat a separate dry skillet over medium heat, add the chorizo slices, and cook, turning occasionally, until lightly browned. Remove with a slotted spoon and drain on paper towels.

Mix the tomato and harissa paste together in a small bowl. Divide the herb salad between 2 plates, spoon over the bean mixture, and sprinkle over the warm chorizo slices. Top with a spoonful of the tomato and harissa mixture and serve immediately.

turkey & rice salad

serves 4

ingredients

4 cups chicken stock
1 cup mixed long-grain and wild rice
2 tbsp vegetable oil
8 oz skinless, boneless turkey breast, trimmed of all visible fat and cut into thin strips
2 cups snow peas
4 oz oyster mushrooms, torn into pieces
1/4 cup shelled pistachio nuts, finely chopped
2 tbsp chopped fresh cilantro
1 tbsp snipped fresh garlic chives
salt and pepper, to taste
1 tbsp balsamic vinegar
fresh garlic chives, to garnish

Bring 1 cup of chicken stock to a boil in a large pan. Add the rice, and cook for 30 minutes, or until tender. Drain and let cool slightly.

Meanwhile, heat 1 tablespoon of the oil in a preheated wok or skillet. Stir-fry the turkey over medium heat for 3–4 minutes, or until cooked through. Using a slotted spoon, transfer the turkey to a serving dish. Add the snow peas and mushrooms to the wok and stir-fry for 1 minute. Add the remaining chicken stock, bring to a boil, then reduce the heat, cover, and let simmer for 3–4 minutes. Transfer the vegetables to the dish and let cool slightly.

Thoroughly mix the rice, turkey, snow peas, mushrooms, nuts, cilantro, and garlic chives together, then season with salt and pepper. Drizzle with the remaining vegetable oil and the vinegar, and garnish with fresh garlic chives. Serve warm.

smoked chicken & cranberry salad

serves 4

ingredients

1 smoked chicken, about 3 lb

1 cup dried cranberries

2 tbsp apple juice or water

7 oz sugar snap peas

2 ripe avocados

juice of ½ lemon

4 lettuce hearts

1 bunch watercress, trimmed

2 oz arugula

for the dressing

2 tbsp olive oil

1 tbsp walnut oil

2 tbsp lemon juice

1 tbsp chopped fresh mixed herbs, such as parsley and lemon thyme

salt and pepper, to taste

Carve the chicken carefully, slicing the white meat. Divide the legs into thighs and drumsticks, and trim the wings. Cover with plastic wrap and refrigerate.

Put the cranberries in a bowl. Stir in the apple juice, then cover with plastic wrap and let soak for 30 minutes.

Meanwhile, blanch the sugar snap peas, then rinse under cold running water, and drain.

Peel, pit, and slice the avocados, and toss in the lemon juice to prevent discoloration.

Separate the lettuce hearts and arrange on a large serving platter with the avocados, sugar snap peas, watercress, arugula, and the chicken.

Put all the dressing ingredients in a screw-top jar, and shake until well blended.

Drain the cranberries and mix them with the dressing, then pour over the salad. Serve immediately.

melon, chorizo & artichoke salad

serves 8

ingredients

12 small globe artichokes
juice of 1/2 lemon
2 tbsp olive oil
1 small orange-fleshed melon, such as cantaloupe
7 oz chorizo sausage, outer casing removed
fresh tarragon or flat-leaf parsley sprigs, to garnish

for the dressing

3 tbsp Spanish extra-virgin olive oil
1 tbsp red wine vinegar
1 tsp prepared mustard
1 tbsp chopped fresh tarragon
salt and pepper, to taste

Prepare the artichokes then brush the cut surfaces of the artichokes with lemon juice to prevent discoloration. Carefully remove the choke (the mass of silky hairs) by pulling it out with your fingers or by scooping it out with a spoon. (It is very important to remove all the choke on older artichokes, as the little barbs, if eaten, can irritate the throat.) Cut the artichokes into quarters and brush them again with lemon juice.

Heat the olive oil in a large, heavy-bottom skillet. Add the prepared artichokes and cook, stirring frequently for 5 minutes or until the artichoke leaves are golden brown. Remove from the skillet, then transfer to a large serving bowl and let cool.

To prepare the melon, cut in half and scoop out the seeds with a spoon. Cut the flesh into bite-size cubes. Add to the cooled artichokes. Cut the chorizo into bite-size chunks and add to the melon and artichokes.

To make the dressing, place all the ingredients in a small bowl, and whisk together. Just before serving, pour the dressing over the prepared salad ingredients and toss together. Serve the salad garnished with tarragon or parsley sprigs.

layered chicken salad

serves 4

ingredients

1 lb 10 oz new potatoes
1 red bell pepper, halved and seeded
1 green bell pepper, halved and seeded
2 small zucchini, sliced
1 small onion, thinly sliced
3 tomatoes, sliced
12 oz cooked chicken, sliced
chopped fresh chives, to garnish

for the dressing

2/3 cup plain yogurt
3 tbsp mayonnaise
1 tbsp chopped fresh chives
salt and pepper, to taste

Preheat the broiler. Put the potatoes into a large pan, add just enough cold water to cover, and bring to a boil. Lower the heat, cover, and simmer for 15–20 minutes until tender. Meanwhile, place the bell pepper halves, skin side up, under the hot broiler, and broil until the skins blacken and begin to char.

Remove the bell peppers with tongs, place in a bowl, and cover with plastic wrap. Set aside until cool enough to handle, then peel off the skins, and slice.

Bring a small pan of lightly salted water to a boil. Add the zucchini, bring back to a boil, and simmer for 3 minutes. Drain, rinse under cold running water to prevent any further cooking, and drain again. Set aside.

To make the dressing, whisk the yogurt, mayonnaise, and chopped chives together in a small bowl until well blended. Season with salt and pepper.

When the potatoes are tender, drain, cool, and slice them. Add them to the dressing, and mix gently to coat evenly. Spoon the potatoes onto 4 serving plates, dividing them equally.

Top each plate with one quarter of the bell pepper slices and zucchini. Layer one quarter of the onion and tomato slices, then the sliced chicken, on top of each serving. Garnish with chopped chives, and serve immediately.

rare roast beef pasta salad

serves 4

ingredients

1 lb round or sirloin steak

salt and pepper, to taste

4 cups fusilli

4 tbsp olive oil

2 tbsp lime juice

2 tbsp Thai fish sauce

2 tsp honey

4 scallions, sliced

1 cucumber, peeled and cut into 1-inch chunks

3 tomatoes, cut into wedges

1 tbsp fresh mint, finely chopped

Season the steak with salt and pepper. Broil or pan-fry it for 4 minutes on each side, or as desired. Let rest for 5 minutes, then slice thinly across the grain.

Meanwhile, bring a large pan of lightly salted water to a boil. Add the pasta, bring back to a boil, and cook for 8–10 minutes or until tender, but still firm to the bite. Drain the pasta, rinse in cold water, and drain again thoroughly. Toss the pasta in the olive oil, and set aside until required.

Combine the lime juice, fish sauce, and honey in a small pan and cook over medium heat for 2 minutes.

Add the scallions, cucumber, tomatoes, and mint to the pan, then add the steak and mix well. Season with salt.

Transfer the fusilli to a large, warm serving dish and top with the steak and salad mixture. Serve warm or let cool completely.

roast duck salad

serves 4

ingredients

2 duck breasts

2 Boston lettuces, shredded

1 cup bean sprouts

1 yellow bell pepper, seeded and cut into thin strips

½ cucumber, seeded and cut into short thin sticks

2 tsp shredded lime zest, to garnish

2 tbsp shredded coconut, toasted, to garnish

for the dressing

juice of 2 limes

3 tbsp Thai fish sauce

1 tbsp soft brown sugar

2 tsp sweet chili sauce

1 inch fresh gingerroot, finely grated

3 tbsp chopped fresh mint

3 tbsp chopped fresh basil

Preheat the oven to 400°F. Place the duck breasts on a rack set over a roasting pan and roast in the oven for 20–30 minutes, or until cooked as desired and the skin is crisp. Remove from the oven and set aside to cool.

In a large bowl, combine the lettuce, bean sprouts, bell pepper, and cucumber. Cut the cooled duck into slices and add to the salad. Mix well.

In a bowl, whisk together the lime juice, fish sauce, brown sugar, chili sauce, gingerroot, mint, and basil. Add the dressing to the salad, and toss well.

Transfer the salad to a serving platter, and garnish with the lime zest and shredded coconut before serving.

warm mushroom, spinach & pancetta salad

serves 4

ingredients

generous 6 cups fresh baby spinach leaves

2 tbsp olive oil

5½ oz pancetta

10 oz mixed wild mushrooms, sliced

for the dressing

5 tbsp olive oil

1 tbsp balsamic vinegar

1 tsp dijon mustard

pinch of sugar

salt and pepper, to taste

To make the dressing, place the olive oil, vinegar, mustard, sugar, salt, and pepper in a small bowl and whisk together. Rinse the baby spinach under cold running water, then drain and place in a large salad bowl.

Heat the oil in a large skillet. Add the pancetta and cook for 3 minutes. Add the mushrooms and cook for 3–4 minutes, or until tender.

Pour the dressing into the skillet and immediately pour the cooked mixture and dressing into the bowl with the spinach. Toss until coated with the dressing and serve immediately.

crispy spinach & bacon salad

serves 4

ingredients

4 tbsp olive oil

4 strips of lean bacon, diced

1 thick slice of white bread, crusts removed, cut into cubes

1 lb fresh spinach, torn or shredded

Heat 2 tablespoons of the olive oil over high heat in a large skillet. Add the diced bacon to the skillet, and cook for 3–4 minutes, or until crisp. Remove with a slotted spoon, place onto paper towels, and set aside.

Toss the cubes of bread in the fat remaining in the skillet over high heat for about 4 minutes, or until crisp and golden. Remove the croutons with a slotted spoon, draining carefully, and set them aside.

Add the remaining olive oil to the skillet and heat. Toss the spinach in the oil over high heat for about 3 minutes, or until it has just wilted. Place the warm spinach in a serving bowl, and sprinkle with the bacon and croutons. Serve immediately.

Thai-style chicken salad

serves 4

ingredients

14 oz small new potatoes, scrubbed and cut in half, lengthwise
7 oz baby corn cobs
1½ cups bean sprouts
3 scallions, trimmed and sliced
4 cooked, skinless chicken breasts, sliced
1 tbsp chopped lemongrass
2 tbsp chopped fresh cilantro
salt and pepper, to taste
1 lime, cut into wedges, to garnish
fresh cilantro leaves, to garnish

for the dressing

6 tbsp chili oil or sesame oil
2 tbsp lime juice
1 tbsp light soy sauce
1 tbsp chopped fresh cilantro
1 small, red chili, seeded and finely sliced

Bring two pans of water to the boil. Put the potatoes into one pan and cook for 15 minutes until tender. Put the corn cobs into the other pan and cook for 5 minutes until tender. Drain the potatoes and corn cobs well and let cool.

When the vegetables are cool, transfer them into a large serving dish. Add the bean sprouts, scallions, chicken, lemongrass, and cilantro and season with salt and pepper.

To make the dressing, put all the ingredients into a bowl, and mix together well. Drizzle the dressing over the salad, and garnish with lime wedges and cilantro leaves. Serve immediately.

duck & radish salad

serves 4

ingredients

12 oz boneless duck breasts

2 tbsp all-purpose flour

salt and pepper, to taste

1 egg

2 tbsp water

2 tbsp sesame seeds

3 tbsp sesame oil

½ head Chinese cabbage, shredded

3 celery stalks, sliced finely

8 radishes, trimmed and halved

fresh basil leaves, to garnish

for the dressing

zest of 1 lime

2 tbsp lime juice

2 tbsp olive oil

1 tbsp light soy sauce

1 tbsp chopped fresh basil

salt and pepper, to taste

Put each duck breast between sheets of baking parchment or plastic wrap. Use a meat mallet or rolling pin to beat them out and flatten them slightly.

Sprinkle the flour onto a large plate and season with salt and pepper. Beat the egg and water together in a shallow bowl, then sprinkle the sesame seeds onto a separate plate.

Dip the duck breasts first into the seasoned flour, then into the egg mixture and finally into the sesame seeds, to coat the duck evenly. Heat the sesame oil in a large preheated skillet.

Fry the duck breasts over medium heat for about 8 minutes, turning once. To test whether they are cooked, insert a sharp knife into the thickest part—the juices should run clear. Lift them out, and drain on paper towels.

To make the dressing, whisk together the lime peel and juice, olive oil, soy sauce, and chopped basil. Season with salt and pepper.

Arrange the Chinese cabbage, celery, and radishes on a serving plate. Slice the duck breasts thinly and place on top of the salad.

Drizzle with the dressing and garnish with fresh basil leaves. Serve immediately.

chicken, cheese & arugula salad

serves 4

ingredients

5½ oz arugula leaves
2 celery stalks, trimmed and sliced
½ cucumber, sliced
2 scallions, trimmed and sliced
2 tbsp chopped fresh parsley
1 oz walnut pieces
12 oz boneless roast chicken, sliced
4½ oz blue cheese, cubed
handful of seedless red grapes, cut in half (optional)
salt and pepper, to taste

for the dressing

2 tbsp olive oil
1 tbsp sherry vinegar
1 tsp dijon mustard
1 tbsp chopped mixed herbs

Place the arugula into a large salad bowl. Add the celery, cucumber, scallions, parsley, and walnuts, and mix together well. Transfer onto a large serving platter. Arrange the chicken slices over the salad, then scatter the cheese on top. Add the red grapes, if using. Season well with salt and pepper.

To make the dressing, put all the ingredients into a bowl, and mix together well. Drizzle the dressing over the salad, and serve.

broiled lamb with yogurt & herb dressing

serves 4

ingredients

2 tbsp sunflower oil, plus extra for broiling the lamb
1 tbsp tomato paste
½ tbsp ground cumin
1 tsp lemon juice
1 garlic clove, crushed
pinch of cayenne pepper
salt and pepper, to taste
1 lb 2 oz lamb neck fillets, trimmed with excess fat removed
toasted sesame seeds and chopped fresh parsley, to garnish

for the dressing

2 tbsp fresh lemon juice
1 tsp honey
3 oz thick plain yogurt
2 tbsp finely shredded fresh mint
2 tbsp chopped fresh parsley
1 tbsp finely snipped fresh chives
salt and pepper, to taste

Mix the 2 tablespoons sunflower oil, tomato paste, cumin, lemon juice, garlic, cayenne, and salt and pepper together in a non-metallic bowl. Add the lamb and rub with the marinade until coated. Cover the bowl and marinate in the refrigerator for at least 2 hours, but ideally overnight.

To make the dressing, whisk the lemon juice and honey together until the honey dissolves. Whisk in the yogurt until well blended. Stir in the herbs and add salt and pepper. Cover and chill until required.

Remove the lamb from the refrigerator 15 minutes before you are ready to cook. Heat the broiler to its highest setting and lightly brush the broiler rack with oil. Broil the lamb, turning it once, for 10 minutes for medium and 12 minutes for well done. Leave the lamb to cool completely, then cover and chill until required.

Thinly slice the lamb, then divide among 4 plates. Adjust the seasoning in the dressing, if necessary, then spoon on top of the lamb slices. Garnish with toasted sesame seeds and parsley and serve.

smoked chicken salad with avocado & tarragon dressing

serves 4–6

ingredients

2 large tomatoes, sliced

1 lb 5 oz smoked chicken, skinned and cut into slices

9 oz fresh watercress, any thick stems or yellow leaves removed, then rinsed and patted dry

3 oz fresh bean sprouts, soaked for 20 minutes in cold water, then drained well and patted dry

leaves from several sprigs of fresh flat-leaf parsley or cilantro

for the dressing

1 ripe, soft avocado

2 tbsp lemon juice

1 tbsp tarragon vinegar

3 oz thick plain yogurt

1 small garlic clove, crushed

1 tbsp chopped fresh tarragon leaves

salt and pepper, to taste

To make the dressing, put the avocado, lemon juice, and vinegar in a blender or food processor and blend until smooth, scraping down the side with a rubber spatula. Add the yogurt, garlic, and tarragon leaves and process again. Season with salt and pepper, then transfer to a bowl. Cover with plastic wrap, and chill for 2 hours.

To assemble the salad, divide the tomato slices among 4–6 individual plates. Toss the smoked chicken, watercress, bean sprouts, and parsley or cilantro leaves together. Divide the salad ingredients among the plates.

Adjust the seasoning in the dressing, if necessary. Spoon the dressing over each salad, and serve.

roast pork & pumpkin salad

serves 4–6

ingredients

1 small pumpkin, about 3½ lbs
2 red onions, cut into wedges
olive oil
3½ oz green beans, topped and tailed and cut in half
1¼ lbs roast pork, any skin or rind removed and cut into bite-size chunks
large handful fresh arugula leaves
3½ oz feta cheese, drained and crumbled
2 tbsp toasted pine nuts
2 tbsp chopped fresh parsley
salt and pepper, to taste

for the vinaigrette

6 tbsp extra-virgin olive oil
3 tbsp balsamic vinegar
½ tsp sugar
½ tsp dijon mustard
salt and pepper, to taste

Preheat the oven to 400°F. Cut the pumpkin in half, scoop out the seeds and fibers, and cut the flesh into wedges about 1½ inches wide. Very lightly rub the pumpkin and onion wedges with the olive oil, place in a roasting pan, and roast for 25–30 minutes, until the pumpkin and onions are tender but holding their shape.

Meanwhile, bring a small pan of salted water to a boil. Add the green beans and blanch for 5 minutes, or until tender. Drain well, and cool under cold running water to stop the cooking. Drain, and pat dry.

Remove the pumpkin and onion wedges from the oven when as they are tender, and let cool completely. When the pumpkin is cool, peel and cut into bite-size pieces.

To make the vinaigrette, put the olive oil, vinegar, sugar, mustard, and salt and pepper into a screw-top jar, and shake until blended.

Toss the pumpkin, onions, green beans, pork, arugula, feta, pine nuts, and parsley in a large bowl and gently toss together, being careful not to break up the pumpkin. Shake the dressing again, pour over the salad, and gently toss. Divide among individual bowls, and serve.

roast chicken with pesto cream salad

serves 4–6

ingredients

1 lb 5 oz cooked boneless chicken, any skin removed and cut into bite-size chunks

3 celery sticks, chopped

1 x 16 oz jar roasted red bell peppers, drained and sliced

salt and pepper, to taste

iceberg lettuce leaves, to serve

for the pesto cream

5 oz sour cream

about 4 tbsp pesto sauce

To make the pesto cream, put the sour cream into a large bowl, then beat in the pesto sauce. Taste and add more pesto if you want a stronger flavor.

Add the chicken, celery, and bell peppers to the bowl and gently toss together. Add salt and pepper and toss again. Cover and chill until required.

Remove the salad from the refrigerator 10 minutes before serving to return to room temperature. Toss the salad, then divide among individual plates lined with lettuce leaves.

sparkling

a collection of fish and seafood salads

salmon & avocado salad

serves 4

ingredients

1 lb new potatoes

4 salmon steaks, about 4 oz each

1 avocado

juice of 1/2 lemon

1 1/4 cups baby spinach leaves

4 1/2 oz mixed small salad greens, including watercress

12 cherry tomatoes, halved

1/2 cup chopped walnuts

for the dressing

3 tbsp unsweetened clear apple juice

1 tsp balsamic vinegar

freshly ground black pepper, to taste

Cut the new potatoes into bite-size pieces, put into a pan, and cover with cold water. Bring to a boil, then reduce the heat, cover, and let simmer for 10–15 minutes, or until just tender. Drain and keep warm.

Meanwhile, preheat the broiler to medium. Cook the salmon steaks under the preheated broiler for 10–15 minutes, depending on the thickness of the steaks, turning halfway through cooking. Remove from the broiler, and keep warm.

While the potatoes and salmon are cooking, cut the avocado in half, remove and discard the pit, and peel the flesh. Cut the avocado flesh into slices and coat in the lemon juice to prevent it from discoloring.

Toss the spinach leaves and mixed salad greens together in a large serving bowl until combined. Arrange 6 cherry tomato halves on each plate of salad.

Remove and discard the skin and any bones from the salmon. Flake the salmon and divide among the plates, along with the potatoes. Sprinkle the walnuts over the salads.

To make the dressing, mix the apple juice and vinegar together in a small bowl, and season with pepper. Drizzle over the salads and serve immediately.

coconut shrimp with cucumber salad

serves 4

ingredients

1 cup brown basmati rice

½ tsp coriander seeds

2 egg whites, lightly beaten

generous ¾ cup dry unsweetened coconut

24 raw jumbo shrimp, shelled

½ cucumber

4 scallions, thinly sliced lengthwise

1 tsp sesame oil

1 tbsp finely chopped fresh cilantro

Bring a large pan of water to a boil, add the rice, and cook for 25 minutes, or until tender. Drain and keep in a strainer covered with a clean dish towel to absorb the steam.

Meanwhile, soak 8 wooden skewers in cold water for 30 minutes. Crush the coriander seeds in a mortar with a pestle. Heat a nonstick skillet over medium heat, add the crushed coriander seeds, and cook, turning, until they start to color. Place onto a plate and set aside.

Put the egg whites into a shallow bowl and the coconut into a separate bowl. Roll each shrimp first in the egg whites, then in the coconut. Thread onto a skewer. Repeat so that each skewer is threaded with 3 coated shrimp.

Preheat the broiler to high. Using a potato peeler, peel long strips from the cucumber to create ribbons, put into a strainer to drain, then toss with the scallions and sesame oil in a bowl, and set aside.

Cook the shrimp under the preheated broiler for 3–4 minutes on each side, or until slightly browned.

Meanwhile, mix the rice with the toasted coriander seeds and fresh cilantro, and divide this and the cucumber salad among bowls. Serve with the hot shrimp skewers.

tuna & avocado salad

serves 4

ingredients

2 avocados, pitted, peeled, and cubed
9 oz cherry tomatoes, halved
2 red bell peppers, seeded and chopped
1 bunch fresh flat-leaf parsley, chopped
2 garlic cloves, crushed
1 fresh red chili, seeded and finely chopped
juice of ½ lemon
6 tbsp olive oil
pepper, to taste
3 tbsp sesame seeds
4 fresh tuna steaks, about 5½ oz each
8 cooked new potatoes, cubed
arugula leaves and crusty bread, to serve

Toss the avocados, tomatoes, red bell peppers, parsley, garlic, chili, lemon juice, and 2 tablespoons of the oil together in a large bowl. Season with pepper, cover, and let chill in the refrigerator for 30 minutes.

Lightly crush the sesame seeds in a mortar with a pestle. Pour the crushed seeds onto a plate and spread out. Press each tuna steak in turn into the crushed seeds to coat on both sides.

Heat 2 tablespoons of the remaining oil in a skillet, add the potatoes, and cook, stirring frequently for 5–8 minutes or until crisp and brown. Remove from the skillet and drain on paper towels.

Wipe out the skillet, add the remaining oil, and heat over high heat until very hot. Add the tuna steaks, and cook for 3–4 minutes on each side.

To serve, divide the avocado salad among 4 serving plates. Top each with a tuna steak, potatoes, and arugula leaves, and serve with crusty bread.

tomato, salmon & shrimp salad

serves 4

ingredients

several lettuce leaves

4 ripe tomatoes, coarsely chopped

3½ oz smoked salmon

4 oz cherry or baby plum tomatoes, halved

7 oz large cooked shrimp, thawed if frozen

pepper, to taste

for the dressing

1 tbsp dijon mustard

2 tsp superfine sugar

2 tsp red wine vinegar

2 tbsp medium olive oil

few fresh dill sprigs, plus extra to garnish

Place the lettuce leaves around the edge of a shallow bowl, and add all the tomatoes and cherry tomatoes. Using scissors, snip the smoked salmon into strips and sprinkle over the tomatoes, then add the shrimp.

Mix the mustard, sugar, vinegar, and oil together in a small bowl, then tear most of the dill sprigs into it. Mix well, and pour over the salad. Toss well to coat the salad with the dressing. Garnish with the remaining dill, and season with pepper.

lobster salad

serves 2

ingredients

2 raw lobster tails

radicchio leaves

fresh dill sprigs, to garnish

for the lemon-dill mayonnaise

⅔ cup olive oil

1 large egg yolk

zest and juice of 1 large lemon

½ tsp dijon mustard

salt and pepper, to taste

1 tbsp chopped fresh dill

To make the lemon-dill mayonnaise, finely grate half the lemon rind and squeeze the juice. Beat the egg yolk in a small bowl, then beat in the mustard and 1 teaspoon of the lemon juice.

Using a whisk or electric mixer, beat the oil into the egg yolk mixture, drop by drop, until a thick mayonnaise forms. Stir in the lemon rind and 1 tablespoon of the remaining lemon juice.

Season the mayonnaise with salt and pepper and add more lemon juice if desired. Stir in the dill, cover, and let chill in the refrigerator until required.

Bring a large pan of lightly salted water to a boil. Add the lobster tails, return to a boil, and cook for 6 minutes, or until the flesh is opaque and the shells are red. Drain immediately, and let cool.

When cool enough to handle, remove the lobster flesh from the shells, and cut into bite-size pieces. Arrange the radicchio leaves on individual plates, and top with the lobster meat. Place a spoonful of the lemon-dill mayonnaise on the side. Garnish with dill sprigs, and serve.

Russian salad

serves 4

ingredients

4 oz new potatoes
generous 1 cup frozen or shelled fresh fava beans
4 oz baby carrots
4 oz baby corn
4 oz baby turnips
4 oz white mushrooms, cut into matchsticks
12 oz cooked shelled shrimp, deveined
½ cup mayonnaise
1 tbsp lemon juice
2 tbsp bottled capers, drained and rinsed
salt and pepper, to taste
2 tbsp extra-virgin olive oil
2 hard-boiled eggs, shelled and halved
4 canned anchovy fillets, drained and halved, to garnish
paprika, to garnish

Cook the new potatoes, fava beans, carrots, corn, and turnips simultaneously. Cook the potatoes in a large, heavy-bottom pan of lightly salted boiling water for 20 minutes. Cook the fava beans in a small pan of lightly salted water for 3 minutes, then drain, rinse under cold running water, and set aside until required. Cook the carrots, corn, and turnips in a large, heavy-bottom pan of lightly salted boiling water for 6 minutes.

Mix the mushrooms and shrimp together in a bowl. Mix the mayonnaise and lemon juice together in a separate bowl, then fold half the mayonnaise mixture into the shrimp mixture. Fold in the capers and season with salt and pepper.

Drain the mixed vegetables, rinse under cold running water, and place in a bowl. When the potatoes are cooked, drain, rinse under cold running water, and add to the bowl with the mixed vegetables. Pop the fava beans out of their skins by pinching them between your index finger and thumb, and add to the bowl. Drizzle the olive oil on top, and toss to coat. Divide the potatoes and vegetables between serving plates, and top with the shrimp mixture. Place a hard-boiled egg half in the center of each and garnish with the halved anchovies. Dust the eggs with paprika, and serve with the remaining mayonnaise mixture.

seafood salad

serves 4

ingredients

9 oz live mussels
12 oz live scallops, shucked and cleaned
9 oz prepared squid, cut into rings and tentacles
1 red onion, halved and thinly sliced
chopped parsley, to garnish
lemon wedges, to serve

for the dressing

4 tbsp extra-virgin olive oil
2 tbsp white wine vinegar
1 tbsp lemon juice
1 garlic clove, finely chopped
1 tbsp chopped fresh flat-leaf parsley
salt and pepper, to taste

Clean the mussels by scrubbing or scraping the shells and pulling out any beards that are attached to them. Discard any with broken shells or any that refuse to close when tapped. Put the mussels in a colander and rinse well under cold running water. Put them in a large pan with a little water and cook, covered, over a high heat, shaking the pan occasionally, for 3–4 minutes, or until the mussels have opened. Discard any mussels that remain closed. Strain the mussels, reserving the cooking liquid. Rinse the mussels under cold running water, drain, and set aside.

Return the reserved cooking liquid to the pan and bring to a boil, add the scallops and squid, and cook for 3 minutes. Remove from the heat and drain. Rinse under cold running water and drain again. Remove the mussels from their shells. Put them in a bowl with the scallops and squid and let cool. Cover with plastic wrap and chill in the refrigerator for 45 minutes.

Divide the seafood among 4 serving plates and top with the onion. Combine all the dressing ingredients in a small bowl, then drizzle over the salad. Garnish with chopped parsley and lemon wedges to serve.

cantaloupe & crab salad

serves 4

ingredients

12 oz fresh crabmeat, shelled
5 tbsp mayonnaise
2 fl oz plain yogurt
4 tsp extra-virgin olive oil
4 tsp lime juice
1 scallion, finely chopped
4 tsp finely chopped fresh parsley
pinch of cayenne pepper
1 cantaloupe
2 radicchio heads, separated into leaves
fresh parsley sprigs, to garnish

Place the crabmeat in a large bowl. Remove any remaining shell or cartilage, being careful not to break up the meat.

Put the mayonnaise, yogurt, olive oil, lime juice, scallion, parsley, and cayenne pepper into a separate bowl, and mix until thoroughly blended. Fold in the crabmeat.

Cut the melon in half, and remove and discard the seeds. Slice into wedges, then cut off the rind with a sharp knife.

Arrange the melon slices and radicchio leaves in 4 large bowls, then arrange the crabmeat mixture on top. Garnish with a few sprigs of fresh parsley.

shrimp & rice salad

serves 4

ingredients

1 cup mixed long-grain and wild rice

12 oz cooked shelled shrimp

1 mango, peeled, seeded, and diced

4 scallions, sliced

1/4 cup slivered almonds

1 tbsp finely chopped fresh mint

salt and pepper, to taste

for the dressing

1 tbsp extra-virgin olive oil

2 tsp lime juice

1 garlic clove, crushed

1 tsp honey

salt and pepper, to taste

Cook the rice in a large pan of lightly salted boiling water for 35 minutes, or until tender. Drain and transfer to a large bowl, then add the shrimp.

To make the dressing, mix all the ingredients together in a bowl, seasoning with the salt and pepper, and whisk well until thoroughly blended. Pour the dressing over the rice and shrimp mixture and let cool.

Add the mango, scallions, almonds, and mint to the salad and season with pepper. Stir thoroughly, transfer to a large serving dish, and serve.

anchovy & olive salad

serves 4

ingredients

large handful of mixed lettuce leaves

12 cherry tomatoes, halved

20 black olives, pitted and halved

6 canned anchovy fillets, drained and sliced

1 tbsp chopped fresh oregano

wedges of lemon, to garnish

crusty bread rolls, to serve

for the dressing

4 tbsp extra-virgin olive oil

1 tbsp white wine vinegar

1 tbsp lemon juice

1 tbsp chopped fresh flat-leaf parsley

salt and pepper, to taste

To make the dressing, put all the ingredients into a small bowl, seasoning with salt and pepper, and stir until well combined.

To assemble the salad, arrange the lettuce leaves in a serving dish. Scatter the cherry tomatoes on top, followed by the olives, anchovies, and oregano. Drizzle over the dressing.

Transfer to individual plates, garnish with lemon wedges, and serve with crusty bread rolls.

smoked salmon & wild arugula salad

serves 4

ingredients

1¾ oz wild arugula leaves, shredded
1 tbsp chopped fresh flat-leaf parsley
2 scallions, finely diced
2 large avocados
1 tbsp lemon juice
9 oz smoked salmon

for the dressing

⅔ cup mayonnaise
2 tbsp lime juice
finely grated rind of 1 lime
1 tbsp chopped fresh flat-leaf parsley, plus extra sprigs to garnish

Arrange the arugula in 4 individual bowls. Sprinkle with chopped parsley and scallions.

Halve, peel, and pit the avocados and cut into thin slices or small chunks. Brush with the lemon juice to prevent discoloration, then divide among the salad bowls. Cut the smoked salmon into strips, and place on top.

To make the dressing, put the mayonnaise in a bowl, then add the lime juice, lime rind, and chopped parsley. Mix together well. Spoon some of the mayonnaise dressing on top of each salad, and garnish with parsley sprigs.

tuna & herbed fusilli salad

serves 4

ingredients

7 oz dried fusilli
1 red bell pepper, seeded and quartered
1 red onion, sliced
4 tomatoes, sliced
7 oz canned tuna in brine, drained and flaked

for the dressing

6 tbsp basil-flavored oil or extra-virgin olive oil
3 tbsp white wine vinegar
1 tbsp lime juice
1 tsp mustard
1 tsp honey
4 tbsp chopped fresh basil, plus extra sprigs to garnish

Bring a large pan of lightly salted water to a boil. Add the pasta, return to a boil, and cook for 8–10 minutes, until tender but still firm to the bite.

Meanwhile, put the bell pepper quarters under a preheated hot broiler and cook for 10–12 minutes until the skins begin to blacken. Transfer to a plastic bag, seal, and set aside.

Remove the pasta from the heat, drain, and set aside to cool. Remove the bell pepper quarters from the bag, and peel off the skins. Slice the bell pepper into strips.

To make the dressing, put all the dressing ingredients in a large bowl and stir together. Add the pasta, bell pepper strips, onion, tomatoes, and tuna. Toss together gently, then divide among serving bowls. Garnish with basil sprigs and serve.

seafood & spinach salad

serves 4

ingredients

1 lb 2 oz live mussels, soaked and cleaned
3½ oz shrimp, peeled and deveined
12 oz scallops
1 lb 2 oz baby spinach leaves
3 scallions, trimmed and sliced

for the dressing

4 tbsp extra-virgin olive oil
2 tbsp white wine vinegar
1 tbsp lemon juice
1 tsp finely grated lemon zest
1 garlic clove, chopped
1 tbsp grated fresh gingerroot
1 small red chili, de-seeded and diced
1 tbsp chopped fresh cilantro
salt and pepper, to taste

Clean the mussels by scrubbing or scraping the shells and pulling out any beards that are attached to them. Discard any with broken shells or any that refuse to close when tapped. Put the mussels in a colander and rinse well under cold running water. Put the mussels into a large pan with a little water, bring to a boil, and cook over high heat for 4 minutes. Drain and reserve the liquid. Discard any mussels that remain closed. Return the reserved liquid to the pan, and bring to a boil. Add the shrimp and scallops and cook for 3 minutes. Drain. Remove the mussels from their shells. Rinse the mussels, shrimp, and scallops in cold water, drain, and put them in a large bowl. Cool, cover with plastic wrap, and chill for 45 minutes.

Meanwhile, rinse the baby spinach leaves and transfer them to a pan with 4 tablespoons of water. Cook over high heat for 1 minute, transfer to a strainer, refresh under cold running water, and drain.

To make the dressing, put all the ingredients into a small bowl and mix together. Arrange the spinach on serving dishes, then scatter over half of the scallions on top. Add the mussels, shrimp, and scallops, then sprinkle with the remaining scallions. Drizzle the dressing on top, and serve.

Neapolitan seafood salad

serves 4

ingredients

1 lb prepared squid, cut into strips
1 lb 10 oz cooked mussels
1 lb 10 oz cooked cockles in brine
5/8 cup white wine
1 1/2 cups olive oil
2 cups dried campanelle or other small pasta shapes
juice of 1 lemon
1 bunch chives, snipped
1 bunch fresh parsley, finely chopped
salt and pepper, to taste
mixed salad greens
4 large tomatoes, to garnish

Put all of the seafood into a large bowl. Add the wine and 3/4 cup olive oil to the bowl, then refrigerate for 6 hours to marinate.

Put the seafood mixture into a pan and simmer over a low heat for 10 minutes. Set aside to cool.

Bring a large pan of lightly salted water to a boil. Add the pasta and 1 tbsp of the remaining olive oil, and cook until tender, but still firm to the bite. Drain thoroughly and rinse in cold water.

Strain off about half of the cooking liquid from the seafood and discard the rest. Mix in the lemon juice, chives, parsley, and the remaining olive oil. Season with salt and pepper. Add the drained pasta to the seafood.

Arrange the salad greens in a bowl. Spoon the seafood salad into the bowl, garnish with tomatoes, and serve.

mussel salad

serves 4

ingredients

2 red bell peppers, halved and seeded

12 oz cooked, shucked mussels, thawed if frozen

1 head radicchio, shredded

3/4 cup arugula

8 cooked green-lipped mussels in their shells

for the dressing

1 tbsp olive oil

1 tbsp lemon juice

1 tsp finely grated lemon peel

2 tsp honey

1 tsp french mustard

1 tbsp snipped fresh chives

salt and pepper, to taste

Put the bell peppers, skin-side up, on a broiler rack and cook under a preheated broiler for 2–3 minutes, or until the skin is charred and blistered and the flesh is soft. Remove from the broiler with tongs, put into a bowl, and cover with plastic wrap. Set aside for 10 minutes, or until cool enough to handle, then peel off the skins.

Slice the roasted bell peppers into thin strips and put into a bowl. Gently stir in the shucked mussels.

To make the dressing, whisk the oil, lemon juice and peel, honey, mustard, and chives together until well blended. Season with salt and pepper. Add the bell pepper and mussel mixture and toss until coated.

Put the radicchio into a serving bowl with the arugula and toss together.

Arrange the mussel mixture in the center of the leaves with the green-lipped mussels in their shells around the edge of the bowl.

sweet & sour fish salad

serves 4

ingredients

8 oz trout fillets

8 oz whitefish fillets
(such as haddock or cod)

1¼ cups water

1 stem lemongrass

2 lime leaves

1 large red chili

1 bunch scallions, trimmed and shredded

4 oz fresh pineapple flesh, diced

1 small red bell pepper, seeded
and diced

1 bunch watercress, washed and trimmed

fresh snipped chives, to garnish

for the dressing

1 tbsp sunflower oil

1 tbsp rice wine vinegar

pinch of chili powder

1 tsp clear honey

salt and pepper, to taste

Rinse the fish and pat dry, place in a skillet, and add water. Bend the lemongrass in half to bruise it, and add to the skillet with the lime leaves. Prick the chili with a fork and add to the pan. Bring to a boil and simmer for 7–8 minutes. Let cool.

Drain the fish fillets thoroughly, then flake the flesh away from the skin and place it in a bowl. Gently stir in the scallions, pineapple, and bell pepper.

Arrange the washed watercress on 4 serving plates, and spoon the cooked fish mixture on top.

To make the dressing, mix all the ingredients together, seasoning well. Spoon it over the fish, and serve the salad garnished with chives.

chilled shrimp with pineapple & papaya salsa

serves 8

ingredients

4 tbsp vegetable oil

1 fresh red chili, seeded and chopped

1 garlic clove, crushed

48 chilled shrimp

chopped fresh parsley

for the pineapple & papaya salsa

1 large papaya, halved, seeded, peeled, and cut into 1/4-inch dice

1 small pineapple, halved, cored, peeled, and cut into 1/4 inch dice

2 scallions, very finely chopped

1 fresh red chili, or to taste, seeded and finely chopped

1 garlic clove, very finely chopped

2 1/2 tsp lemon juice

1/2 tsp ground cumin

1/4 tsp salt

pepper, to taste

To make the salsa, put the papaya in a large bowl with the pineapple, scallions, chili, garlic, lemon juice, cumin, salt, and pepper. Adjust the lemon juice, cumin, salt, and pepper. Cover and chill until required, ideally at least 2 hours.

Heat a wok over a high heat. Add the vegetable oil and swirl around to coat the wok, then add the chili and garlic and stir-fry for 20 seconds. Add the shrimp and stir-fry for 2–3 minutes until the shrimp are cooked through, become pink, and curl.

Place the shrimp, garlic, and any oil left in the wok in a heatproof bowl, and leave the shrimp to cool and marinate in the chili oil. When the shrimps are completely cool, cover the bowl and chill for at least 2 hours.

When ready to serve, place a spoonful of salsa on each of 8 plates. Remove the shrimp from the marinade, and divide among plates. Sprinkle with parsley and serve.

seared swordfish with fresh tomato salsa

serves 4

ingredients

4 boneless swordfish steaks, about 5 oz each
salt and pepper, to taste
stick of butter
1 tbsp olive oil
slices of crusty bread, to serve

for the fresh tomato & olive salsa

4 tbsp extra-virgin olive oil
1 tbsp red-wine vinegar
1 lb 5 oz ripe, juicy beefsteak tomatoes, cored, seeded, and finely chopped
5 oz large black olives, pitted and cut in half
1 shallot, finely chopped or thinly sliced
1 tbsp capers in brine, rinsed and dried
salt and pepper, to taste
3 tbsp finely shredded fresh basil leaves

To make the fresh tomato & olive salsa, whisk the olive oil and vinegar together in a large bowl. Gently fold in the tomatoes, olives, shallot, capers, salt, and pepper. Cover and chill until required.

Season the swordfish steaks on both sides with salt. Melt the butter with the olive oil in a large skillet. (If you don't have a large enough pan to cook the steaks without overlapping, cook them in 2 batches.)

Fry the steaks for 5 minutes, or until golden brown, then carefully turn the fish over and continue frying about 3 minutes longer, until the fish is cooked through and flakes easily. Remove the fish from the pan and set aside to cool completely. Cover and chill for at least 2 hours.

When ready to serve, remove the fish from the fridge at least 15 minutes in advance. Stir the basil into the salsa, and season to taste. Use a fork to flake the swordfish, and gently stir into the salsa, taking care not to break up the fish too much. Arrange the fish salad in 4 bowls, spooning any of the leftover juices on top. Serve with slices of crusty bread.

shrimp cocktail salad

serves 4

ingredients

2 tsp salt
½ lemon, sliced
32 large shelled and deveined shrimp, defrosted if frozen
6 oz ketchup
1½ tbsp grated horseradish
3 celery sticks, cut into ¼-inch slices
finely grated zest and juice of 1 lemon
salt and pepper, to taste
iceberg lettuce leaves, shredded, to serve
lemon wedges, to garnish

Bring a large pan of water to a rolling boil. Stir in the salt and lemon slices, then reduce the heat to low. Add the shrimp, and leave to simmer for about 3 minutes until they are cooked through, turn pink, and curl. Drain the shrimp into a large colander and immediately rinse with cold running water to stop the cooking and cool the shrimps; set aside.

Combine the ketchup, horseradish, celery, and lemon zest in a bowl and stir together. Stir in 1 tablespoon lemon juice, then add more juice and salt and pepper. Stir in the shrimp, then cover and chill for at least 2 hours.

When ready to serve, stir the shrimp salad and adjust the seasoning, if necessary. Divide the shredded lettuce among 4 glass bowls and spoon the salad on top. Serve immediately while the salad is still chilled, with lemon wedges to garnish.

celery root rémoulade with crab

serves 4

ingredients

1 lb celery root, peeled and grated

juice of 1 lemon

9 oz fresh white crabmeat

chopped fresh dill or parsley, to garnish

for the rémoulade dressing

5 oz mayonnaise

1 tbsp dijon mustard

1½ tsp white wine vinegar

2 tbsp capers in brine, well rinsed

salt and white pepper, to taste

To make the dressing, put the mayonnaise in a bowl. Beat in the mustard, vinegar, and capers, with salt and white pepper—the mixture should be piquant with a strong mustard flavor. Cover and chill until required.

Bring a large pan of salted water to a rolling boil. Add the grated celery root and lemon juice to the water, and blanch for 1½–2 minutes, until it is just slightly tender. Rinse the celery root well, then put it under cold running water to stop the cooking. Use your hands to squeeze out the excess moisture, then pat the celery root dry with paper towels or a clean kitchen towel.

Stir the celery root into the dressing, along with the crabmeat. Taste and adjust the seasoning, if necessary. Cover and chill for at least 30 minutes.

When ready to serve, spoon into bowls and garnish with dill or parsley.

tuna Niçoise

serves 4

ingredients

2 tuna steaks, about 3/4 inch thick

olive oil, for brushing

salt and pepper, to taste

9 oz green beans, trimmed

1/2 cup vinaigrette or garlic vinaigrette dressing

2 hearts of lettuce, leaves separated

3 large hard-boiled eggs, cut into fourths

2 juicy vine-ripened tomatoes, cut into wedges

1 3/4 oz anchovy fillets in oil, drained

2 oz Niçoise olives, pitted

Heat a ridged cast-iron grill pan over high heat, until you can feel the heat rising from the surface. Brush the tuna steaks with oil, place oiled side down on the hot pan, and cook for 2 minutes. Lightly brush the top sides of the tuna steaks with more oil. Turn the tuna steaks over, then season with salt and pepper. Continue cooking for another 2 minutes for rare or up to 4 minutes for well done. Let cool.

Meanwhile, bring a pan of salted water to a boil. Add the beans to the pan and return to a boil, then boil for 3 minutes, or until tender-crisp. Drain the beans, and immediately transfer them to a large bowl. Pour the vinaigrette over the beans, and stir together, then let the beans cool in the dressing.

To serve, line a platter with lettuce leaves. Lift the beans out of the bowl, leaving the excess dressing behind, and place them in the center of the platter. Break the tuna into large pieces and arrange it over the beans. Arrange the hard-boiled eggs and the tomatoes around the side. Arrange the anchovy fillets and olives over the salad. Drizzle the remaining dressing over the salad, and serve.

lentil & tuna salad

serves 4

ingredients

2 ripe tomatoes, finely diced

1 small red onion, finely chopped

14 oz can lentils, drained

6½ oz can tuna, drained

2 tbsp chopped fresh cilantro

pepper, to taste

for the dressing

3 tbsp virgin olive oil

1 tbsp lemon juice

1 tsp whole-grain mustard

1 garlic clove, crushed

½ tsp ground cumin

½ tsp ground coriander

To make the dressing, whisk together the virgin olive oil, lemon juice, mustard, garlic, cumin, and coriander in a small bowl until thoroughly combined. Set aside until required.

Mix together the tomatoes, onion, and drained lentils in a large bowl.

Flake the tuna with a fork and stir it into the onion, tomato, and lentil mixture. Stir in the chopped fresh cilantro, and mix well.

Pour the dressing over the lentil and tuna salad, and season with pepper. Serve immediately.

tuna & two-bean salad

serves 4

ingredients

7 oz green beans

14 oz canned white beans, such as cannellini, rinsed and drained

4 scallions, finely chopped

2 fresh tuna steaks, about 8 oz each and 3/4 inch thick

olive oil, for brushing

salt and pepper, to taste

9 oz cherry tomatoes, halved

lettuce leaves

fresh mint and parsley sprigs, to garnish

for the dressing

handful of fresh mint leaves, shredded

handful of fresh parsley leaves, chopped

1 garlic clove, crushed

4 tbsp extra-virgin olive oil

1 tbsp red wine vinegar

salt and pepper, to taste

First, make the dressing. Put the mint leaves, parsley leaves, garlic, olive oil, red wine vinegar, salt, and pepper into a screw-top jar, and shake until blended. Pour into a large bowl, and set aside.

Bring a pan of lightly salted water to a boil. Add the green beans and cook for 3 minutes. Add the white beans and cook for another 4 minutes until the green beans are tender-crisp and the white beans are heated through. Drain well, and add to the bowl with the dressing and scallions. Toss together.

To cook the tuna, heat a stove top ridged grill pan over high heat. Lightly brush the tuna steaks with oil, then season with salt and pepper. Cook the steaks for 2 minutes, then turn over and cook on the other side for an additional 2 minutes for rare or up to 4 minutes for well done.

Remove the tuna from the grill pan and leave to rest for 2 minutes, or alternatively leave until completely cool. When ready to serve, add the tomatoes to the bean mixture and toss lightly. Line a serving platter with lettuce leaves and top with the bean salad. Place the tuna on top. Serve warm or at room temperature, garnished with herbs.

tuna & fresh vegetable salad

serves 4

ingredients

12 cherry tomatoes, halved

1½ cups whole green beans, cut into 1-inch pieces

8 oz zucchini, thinly sliced

3¼ cups thinly sliced white mushrooms

salad greens

12 oz canned tuna in brine, drained and flaked

fresh parsley, to garnish

for the dressing

4 tbsp mayonnaise

4 tbsp plain yogurt

2 tbsp white wine vinegar

salt and pepper, to taste

To make the dressing, put the mayonnaise, yogurt, vinegar, salt, and pepper in a screw-top jar and shake together until the ingredients are well blended.

Combine the tomatoes, beans, zucchini, and mushrooms in a bowl. Pour over the dressing and marinate for about 1 hour.

Arrange the salad greens on a serving dish. Add the vegetables and tuna, and garnish with parsley.

shrimp & mango salad

serves 4

ingredients

2 mangoes

2 cups peeled, cooked shrimp

salad greens, to serve

4 whole cooked shrimp, to garnish

for the dressing

juice from the mangoes

6 tbsp plain yogurt

2 tbsp mayonnaise

1 tbsp lemon juice

salt and pepper, to taste

Cutting close to the pit, cut a large slice from one side of each mango, then cut another slice from the opposite side. Without breaking the skin, cut the flesh in the segments into squares, then push the skin inside out to expose the cubes, and cut away from the skin. Use a sharp knife to peel the remaining center section and cut the flesh away from the pit into cubes. Reserve any juice in a bowl and put the diced fruit in a separate bowl.

Blend together the mango juice, yogurt, mayonnaise, lemon juice, salt, and pepper.

Arrange the salad greens on a serving dish and add the diced mango and shrimp. Pour the dressing over them, and serve garnished with the whole shrimp.

health-boosting

a collection of energizing salads

wild rice salad with cucumber & orange

serves 4

ingredients

$1\frac{1}{3}$ cups wild rice

$3\frac{1}{2}$ cups water

1 each red, yellow, and orange bell peppers, skinned, seeded, and thinly sliced

½ cucumber, halved lengthwise and sliced

1 orange, peeled, pith removed, and cubed

3 ripe tomatoes, cut into chunks

1 red onion, very finely chopped

generous handful of chopped flat-leaf parsley

for the dressing

1 clove garlic, crushed

1 tbsp balsamic vinegar

2 tbsp extra-virgin olive oil

salt and pepper, to taste

Put the wild rice and water into a large pan and bring to a boil. Stir, then cover and simmer for 40 minutes, or until the rice is firm to the bite. Uncover the rice for the last few minutes of cooking to let any excess water evaporate.

To make the dressing, put the crushed garlic, balsamic vinegar, olive oil, and seasoning into a screw-top jar and shake vigorously. Add extra vinegar, oil, or seasoning as required.

Drain the rice and place in a large bowl. Pour the dressing on top, and mix in. Then mix in the chopped bell peppers, cucumber, orange, tomatoes, red onion, and flat-leaf parsley, and serve.

red bell pepper & radicchio salad

serves 4

ingredients

2 red bell peppers, de-seeded and cut into rings
1 head radicchio, separated into leaves
4 cooked whole beets, cut into matchsticks
12 radishes, sliced
4 scallions, finely chopped
4 tbsp vinaigrette

Arrange the radicchio leaves in a salad bowl. Add the bell pepper, beets, radishes, and scallions. Drizzle with the vinaigrette, and serve.

spring clean salad

serves 4

ingredients

2 dessert apples, cored and diced
juice of 1 lemon
large chunk of watermelon, seeded and cubed
1 head endive, sliced into rounds
4 sticks celery with leaves, coarsely chopped
1 tbsp walnut oil

Place the apples in a bowl and pour the lemon juice on top. Mix well to prevent discoloration.

Add the rest of the fruit and vegetables to the bowl and mix gently. Pour in the walnut oil, mix, and serve.

chickpea & tomato salad

serves 4

ingredients

6 oz dried chickpeas or
 1½ cups canned, drained and rinsed
2–3 ripe tomatoes, coarsely chopped
1 red onion, thinly sliced
handful of fresh basil leaves, torn
1 romaine lettuce, torn

for the dressing

1 green chili, seeded and finely chopped
1 garlic clove, crushed
juice and zest of 2 lemons
2 tbsp olive oil
1 tbsp water
pepper, to taste

If using dried chickpeas, soak overnight, then boil for 30 minutes, or until soft. Let cool.

To make the dressing, put the chili, garlic, lemon juice and zest, olive oil, water, and pepper in a screw-top jar and shake vigorously. Taste and add more lemon juice or oil if necessary.

Add the tomatoes, onion, and basil to the chickpeas, and mix gently. Pour the dressing on top, and mix again. Arrange on a bed of lettuce, and serve.

fennel & orange salad

serves 4

ingredients

2 oranges, peeled and sliced

1 bulb fennel, thinly sliced

1 red onion, peeled and sliced into thin rings

for the dressing

juice of 1 orange

2 tbsp balsamic vinegar

Arrange the orange slices in the bottom of a shallow dish. Place a layer of fennel on top and then add a layer of onion.

Mix the orange juice with the vinegar and drizzle over the salad.

warm new potato & lentil salad

serves 4

ingredients

3/8 cup puy lentils

1 lb new potatoes

6 scallions, thinly sliced

1 tbsp olive oil

2 tbsp balsamic vinegar

salt and pepper, to taste

Bring a large pan of water to a boil. Rinse the lentils, then cook for 20 minutes, or until tender. Drain and rinse, then put to one side.

Meanwhile, steam or boil the potatoes until they are tender. Drain and halve.

Put the lentils, potatoes, and scallions into a serving dish and toss with the olive oil and balsamic vinegar. Season with salt and pepper.

bean sprout, apricot & almond salad

serves 4

ingredients

1⅔ cups bean sprouts, washed and dried
small bunch seedless black and green grapes, halved
12 unsulfured dried apricots, halved
¼ cup blanched almonds, halved
freshly ground pepper, to taste

for the dressing

1 tbsp walnut oil
1 tsp sesame oil
2 tsp balsamic vinegar

Place the bean sprouts in the bottom of a large salad bowl, and sprinkle the grapes and apricots on top.

Place the oils and vinegar in a screw-top jar and shake vigorously to mix. Pour over the salad.

Garnish with the almonds, and season with freshly ground pepper.

asparagus & tomato salad

serves 4

ingredients

8 oz asparagus spears

1 lamb's lettuce, washed and torn

1 handful arugula or mizuna leaves

1 lb ripe tomatoes, sliced

12 black olives, pitted and chopped

1 tbsp toasted pine nuts

for the dressing

1 tsp lemon oil

1 tbsp olive oil

1 tsp whole-grain mustard

2 tbsp balsamic vinegar

sea salt and pepper, to taste

Steam the asparagus spears for 8 minutes, or until tender. Rinse under cold running water to prevent them cooking any further, then cut into 2-inch pieces.

Arrange the lettuce and arugula or mizuna leaves around a salad platter to form the base of the salad. Place the sliced tomatoes in a circle on top and the asparagus in the center. Sprinkle the black olives and pine nuts on top.

Put the lemon oil, olive oil, mustard, and vinegar in a screw-top jar and season with sea salt and black pepper. Shake vigorously, and drizzle over the salad.

avocado salad

serves 4

ingredients

large handful of radicchio
large handful of arugula
1 small galia melon
2 ripe avocados
1 tbsp lemon juice
7 oz fontina cheese,
cut into bite-size pieces

for the dressing

5 tbsp lemon-flavored or
extra-virgin olive oil
1 tbsp white wine vinegar
1 tbsp lemon juice
1 tbsp chopped fresh parsley

To make the dressing, mix together the olive oil, white wine vinegar, lemon juice, and parsley in a small bowl.

Arrange the radicchio and arugula on serving plates. Cut the melon in half, then seed it, and cut the flesh away from the skin. Discard the skin. Slice the melon flesh, and arrange it over the salad greens.

Cut the avocados in half and remove and discard the pits and skin. Slice the flesh and brush with lemon juice. Arrange the slices over the melon, then sprinkle the cheese on top. Drizzle the dressing over the salad, and serve.

herby potato salad

serves 4–6

ingredients

1 lb 2 oz new potatoes

salt and pepper, to taste

16 vine-ripened cherry tomatoes, halved

generous 3/8 cup black olives, pitted and coarsely chopped

4 scallions, finely sliced

2 tbsp chopped fresh mint

2 tbsp chopped fresh parsley

2 tbsp chopped fresh cilantro

juice of 1 lemon

3 tbsp extra-virgin olive oil

Cook the potatoes in a pan of lightly salted boiling water for 15 minutes, or until tender. Drain, then let cool slightly before peeling off the skins. Cut into halves or fourths, depending on the size of the potato. Then combine with the tomatoes, olives, scallions, and herbs in a salad bowl.

Mix the lemon juice and oil together in a small bowl or pitcher, and pour over the potato salad. Season with salt and pepper before serving.

tabbouleh salad

serves 4

ingredients

1 cup quinoa

$2\frac{1}{2}$ cups water

10 vine-ripened cherry tomatoes, seeded and halved

3-inch piece cucumber, diced

3 scallions, finely chopped

juice of $\frac{1}{2}$ lemon

2 tbsp extra-virgin olive oil

4 tbsp chopped fresh mint

4 tbsp chopped fresh cilantro

4 tbsp chopped fresh parsley

salt and pepper, to taste

Put the quinoa into a medium-size pan, and cover with the water. Bring to a boil, then reduce the heat, cover, and let simmer over low heat for 15 minutes. Drain if necessary.

Let the quinoa cool slightly before combining with the cherry tomatoes, cucumber, scallions, lemon juice, and olive oil in a salad bowl. Season with fresh mint, cilantro, and parsley and salt and pepper before serving.

buckwheat noodle and smoked tofu salad

serves 2

ingredients

7 oz buckwheat noodles
9 oz firm smoked tofu (drained weight)
7 oz white cabbage, finely shredded
9 oz carrots, finely shredded
3 scallions, diagonally sliced
1 fresh red chili, seeded and finely sliced into circles
2 tbsp sesame seeds, lightly toasted

for the dressing

1 tsp grated fresh gingerroot
1 garlic clove, crushed
6 oz silken tofu (drained weight)
4 tsp tamari (wheat-free soy sauce)
2 tbsp sesame oil
4 tbsp hot water
salt, to taste

Cook the noodles in a large pan of lightly salted boiling water according to the package instructions. Drain and rinse under cold running water.

To make the dressing, blend the gingerroot, garlic, silken tofu, tamari, sesame oil, and water together in a small bowl until smooth and creamy. Season with salt.

Place the smoked tofu in a steamer. Steam for 5 minutes, then cut into thin slices.

Meanwhile, put the cabbage, carrots, scallions, and chili into a bowl, and toss to mix. To serve, arrange the noodles on serving plates and top with the carrot salad and slices of tofu. Spoon the dressing on top, and garnish with sesame seeds.

zucchini & mint salad

serves 4

ingredients

2 zucchini, cut into thin sticks

3½ oz green beans, cut into thirds

1 green bell pepper, seeded and cut into strips

2 celery stalks, sliced

1 bunch of watercress

for the dressing

1 cup plain yogurt

1 garlic clove, crushed

2 tbsp chopped fresh mint

pepper, to taste

Cook the zucchini and beans in a pan of lightly salted water for 7–8 minutes. Drain, rinse under cold running water, and drain again. Let cool completely.

Mix the zucchini and beans with the green bell pepper strips, celery, and watercress in a large serving bowl.

To make the dressing, combine the yogurt, garlic, and mint in a small bowl. Season with pepper.

Spoon the dressing onto the salad, and serve immediately.

tomato, mozzarella & avocado salad

serves 4

ingredients

2 ripe beefsteak tomatoes, cut into wedges

3½ oz mozzarella cheese

2 avocados

few fresh basil leaves, torn into pieces

20 black olives

for the dressing

1 tbsp olive oil

1½ tbsp white wine vinegar

1 tsp coarse grain mustard

salt and pepper, to taste

Place the tomato wedges in a large serving dish. Drain the mozzarella cheese and coarsely tear into pieces. Cut the avocados in half and remove the pits. Cut the flesh into slices, then arrange the mozzarella cheese and avocado with the tomatoes.

Mix the oil, vinegar, and mustard together in a small bowl, add salt and pepper, then drizzle over the salad.

Sprinkle the basil and olives over the top, and serve immediately.

roasted vegetable salad

serves 4

ingredients

1 onion

1 eggplant, about 8 oz

1 red bell pepper, seeded

1 orange bell pepper, seeded

1 large zucchini, about 6 oz

2–4 garlic cloves

2–4 tbsp olive oil

salt and pepper, to taste

1 tbsp shredded fresh basil

freshly shaved Parmesan cheese

fresh crusty bread, to serve

for the dressing

1 tbsp balsamic vinegar

2 tbsp extra-virgin olive oil

salt and pepper, to taste

Preheat the oven to 400°F. Cut all the vegetables into even-size wedges, put into a roasting pan, and sprinkle over the garlic.

Pour 2 tablespoons of the olive oil over the vegetables, and turn them in the oil until well coated. Season with salt and pepper. Roast in the preheated oven for 40 minutes, or until tender, adding the extra olive oil if becoming too dry.

Meanwhile, put the balsamic vinegar, extra-virgin olive oil, and salt and pepper into a screw-top jar, and shake until blended.

Once the vegetables are cooked, remove from the oven, arrange on a serving dish, and pour the dressing on top. Sprinkle with the basil and shavings of Parmesan cheese. Serve warm or cold with fresh crusty bread.

three bean salad

serves 4–6

ingredients

6 oz mixed salad greens, such as spinach, arugula, and frisée
1 red onion, halved and thinly sliced
3 oz radishes, thinly sliced
6 oz cherry tomatoes, halved
4 oz cooked beet, diced
10 oz canned cannellini beans, drained and rinsed
7 oz canned red kidney beans, drained and rinsed
10½ oz canned flageolet beans, drained and rinsed
⅓ cup dried cranberries
½ cup roasted cashews
8 oz feta cheese (drained weight), crumbled

for the dressing

4 tbsp extra-virgin olive oil
1 tsp dijon mustard
2 tbsp lemon juice
1 tbsp chopped fresh cilantro
salt and pepper, to taste

Arrange the salad greens in a salad bowl and set aside.

In a bowl, combine the onion, radishes, tomatoes, beet, beans, and cranberries.

Put all the dressing ingredients into a screw-top jar, and shake until blended. Pour the dressing over the bean mixture, toss lightly, then spoon on top of the salad greens.

Sprinkle the nuts and cheese over the salad, and serve immediately.

succotash salad

serves 4–6

ingredients

1 tbsp apple cider vinegar
1 tsp whole-grain mustard
1 tsp sugar
3 tbsp garlic-flavored olive oil
1 tbsp sunflower oil
14 oz canned corn kernels, rinsed and drained
14 oz string beans, finely chopped
2 peeled red bell peppers from a jar, drained and finely chopped
2 scallions, very finely chopped
salt and pepper, to taste
2 tbsp chopped fresh parsley, to garnish

Beat the apple cider vinegar, mustard, and sugar together. Gradually whisk in the olive and sunflower oils to form an emulsion.

Stir in the corn kernels, string beans, bell peppers, and scallions. Add salt and pepper. Cover and chill for up to one day.

When ready to serve, adjust the seasoning, if necessary, and garnish with parsley.

spinach salad with blue cheese dressing

serves 4–6

ingredients

10 oz bag baby spinach leaves, any thick stems or yellow leaves removed, then well rinsed and dried
4 scallions, chopped
3 oranges, segmented
2 oz sunflower seeds

for the blue cheese dressing

4 oz full-flavored blue cheese, such as roquefort, crumbled
7 oz thick plain yogurt
1 tbsp white wine vinegar
½ onion, grated
½ small bunch fresh chives, chopped
salt and pepper, to taste

To make the dressing, put the blue cheese, yogurt, vinegar, and onion in a blender or food processor, and blend until smooth. Add the chives and give another quick blitz. Season with salt and pepper. Cover and chill until required.

Place the spinach leaves and scallions in a salad bowl, and toss with half the dressing. Transfer to a serving bowl and top with the orange segments and a sprinkling of sunflower seeds.

pear & roquefort salad

serves 4

ingredients

few leaves of red leaf lettuce
few leaves of radicchio
few leaves of mâche
2 ripe pears, sliced lengthwise
whole fresh chives, to garnish

for the dressing

2 oz roquefort cheese
2/3 cup plain yogurt
2 tbsp chopped fresh chives
pepper, to taste

To make the dressing, place the cheese in a bowl, and mash with a fork. Gradually blend the yogurt into the cheese to make a smooth dressing. Add the chives and season with pepper.

Tear the red leaf lettuce, radicchio, and mâche leaves into 1–2-inch pieces. Arrange the salad greens on a large serving platter or divide them among individual serving plates. Arrange the pear slices over the salad leaves.

Drizzle the dressing over the pears, and garnish with a few whole chives.

green fruit salad

serves 4

ingredients

1 honeydew melon

2 green apples, chopped

2 kiwi fruit, peeled and sliced

4 oz seedless white grapes

fresh mint sprigs, to garnish

for the syrup dressing

1 orange

2/3 cup white wine

2/3 cup water

4 tbsp honey

fresh mint sprigs

To make the syrup, pare the rind from the orange using a potato peeler.

Put the orange rind in a pan with the white wine, water, and honey. Bring to a boil, then simmer gently for 10 minutes.

Remove the syrup from the heat. Add the mint sprigs and set aside to cool.

To prepare the fruit, first cut the melon in half and scoop out the seeds. Use a melon baller or a teaspoon to make melon balls.

Strain the cooled syrup into a serving bowl, removing and reserving the orange rind, and discarding the mint sprigs.

Add the apple, kiwi fruit, grapes, and melon to the serving bowl. Stir through gently to mix.

Serve the fruit salad, garnished with sprigs of fresh mint and some of the reserved orange rind.

tropical fruit salad

serves 4

ingredients

1 papaya

1 mango

1 pineapple

4 oranges, peeled and cut into segments

4½ oz strawberries, hulled and quartered

light or heavy cream, to serve

for the syrup dressing

6 tbsp superfine sugar

1¾ cups water

½ tsp ground allspice

grated rind of ½ lemon

To make the dressing, put the sugar, water, allspice, and lemon rind into a pan. Bring to a boil, stirring continuously, then continue to boil for 1 minute. Remove from the heat and let cool to room temperature. Transfer to a bowl, cover with plastic wrap, and chill in the refrigerator for at least 1 hour.

Peel and halve the papaya and remove the seeds. Cut the flesh into small chunks or slices, and put into a large bowl. Cut the mango twice lengthwise, close to the pit. Remove and discard the pit. Peel and cut the flesh into small chunks or slices, and add to the bowl. Cut off the top and bottom of the pineapple, and remove the hard peel. Cut the pineapple in half lengthwise, then into quarters, and remove the tough core. Cut the remaining flesh into small pieces and add to the bowl. Add the orange segments and strawberries.

Pour the chilled syrup on top of the fruit, cover with plastic wrap, and chill until required. Serve with light or heavy cream.

fig & watermelon salad

serves 4

ingredients

1 watermelon, weighing about 3 lb 5 oz, cut into 1-inch cubes

3/4 cup black seedless grapes

4 figs, cut into wedges

for the syrup dressing

grated rind of 1 lime

grated rind and juice of 1 orange

1 tbsp maple syrup

2 tbsp honey

Place the watermelon cubes in a bowl with the grapes and fig wedges.

Mix with the lime rind, orange rind and juice, maple syrup, and honey in a small pan. Bring to a boil over low heat. Remove from heat, pour the mixture over the fruit, and stir. Let cool. Stir again, cover, and let chill in the refrigerator for at least 1 hour, stirring occasionally.

Divide the fruit salad equally among 4 bowls, and serve.

melon & mango salad

serves 4

ingredients

1 cantaloupe melon, diced

2 oz black grapes, halved and seeded

2 oz green grapes

1 large mango, diced

1 bunch watercress, trimmed

iceberg lettuce leaves, shredded

1 passion fruit

for the melon dressing

2/3 cup plain yogurt

1 tbsp honey

1 tsp grated fresh gingerroot

for the salad greens dressing

2 tbsp olive oil

1 tbsp apple vinegar

salt and pepper, to taste

To make the melon dressing, whisk together the yogurt, honey, and gingerroot in a small bowl.

Make the dressing for the salad greens by whisking together the olive oil and vinegar with a little salt and pepper. Drizzle over the salad greens.

Place the melon in a bowl with the grapes and mango, and gently mix to combine.

Arrange the watercress and lettuce leaves on 4 serving plates. Divide the melon mixture among the plates, and spoon the yogurt dressing on top.

Scoop the seeds out of the passion fruit and sprinkle them over the salads. Serve immediately.

papaya salad

serves 4

ingredients

1 crisp lettuce

1/4 small white cabbage

2 papayas

2 tomatoes, peeled and sliced

1 oz roasted peanuts, chopped roughly

4 scallions, trimmed and thinly sliced

basil leaves, to garnish

for the dressing

4 tbsp olive oil

1 tbsp Thai fish sauce or light soy sauce

2 tbsp lime or lemon juice

1 tbsp dark brown sugar

1 tsp finely chopped fresh red or green chili

To make the dressing, whisk together the oil, fish sauce or soy sauce, lime or lemon juice, sugar, and chili. Set aside, stirring occasionally to dissolve the sugar.

Shred the lettuce and white cabbage, then toss together and arrange on a large serving plate.

Peel the papayas and slice them in half. Scoop out the seeds, then slice the flesh thinly. Arrange on top of the lettuce and cabbage with the sliced tomatoes.

Sprinkle the peanuts and scallions on top. Whisk the dressing, and pour over the salad. Garnish with basil leaves, and serve immediately.

exotic fruit cocktail

serves 4

ingredients

2 oranges

2 large passion fruit

1 pineapple

1 pomegranate

1 banana

Cut 1 orange in half and squeeze the juice into a bowl, discarding any seeds. Using a sharp knife, cut away all the peel and pith from the second orange. Working over the bowl to catch the juice, carefully cut the orange segments between the membranes to obtain skinless segments of fruit. Discard any seeds.

Cut the passion fruit in half, scoop the flesh into a mesh strainer, and using a spoon, push the pulp and juice into the bowl of orange segments. Discard the seeds.

Using a sharp knife, cut away all the skin from the pineapple and cut the flesh lengthwise into fourths. Cut away the central hard core. Cut the flesh into chunks and add to the orange and passion fruit mixture. Cover and, if you are not serving immediately, let the fruit chill.

Cut the pomegranate into fourths and, using your fingers or a teaspoon, remove the red arils from the membrane. Cover and let chill until ready to serve—do not add too early to the fruit cocktail because the seeds discolor the other fruit.

Just before serving, peel and slice the banana, add to the fruit cocktail with the pomegranate seeds, and mix thoroughly. Serve immediately.

melon & strawberry salad

serves 4

ingredients

1/2 iceberg lettuce, shredded

1 small honeydew melon, chopped into 1-inch pieces

2 cups strawberries, sliced

2-inch piece cucumber, thinly sliced

fresh mint sprigs, to garnish

for the dressing

1 cup plain yogurt

2-inch piece cucumber, peeled

a few fresh mint leaves

1/2 tsp finely grated lime or lemon rind

pinch of superfine sugar

3–4 ice cubes

Arrange the shredded lettuce on 4 serving plates. Place the melon on the beds of lettuce with the strawberry and cucumber slices.

To make the dressing, put the yogurt, cucumber, mint leaves, lime or lemon rind, superfine sugar, and ice cubes into a blender or food processor. Blend together for about 15 seconds until smooth.

Drizzle the dressing over the salad. Garnish with sprigs of fresh mint.

index